English Workbook

AGE 9–11

Reading and Comprehension

Susan Elkin

GALORE PARK

AN HACHETTE UK COMPANY

About the author

Susan Elkin is an award-winning journalist who has taught English in five different secondary schools, both independent and state, over many years, most recently at Benenden. She is the author of over 30 books including *English Year 9* and the *English A* Study Guide* and has been a regular contributor to many newspapers and magazines including the *Daily Telegraph* and *Daily Mail*. She is Education Editor at *The Stage* and writes blogs for *The Independent*. You can read about Susan's early classroom experiences in her 2013 e-book *Please Miss We're Boys*.

The publishers would like to thank the following for permission to reproduce copyright material:

p6 John Steinbeck: from *Travels with Charley: In Search of America* (Penguin Books, 1980); **p9 Edward Lucie-Smith:** 'The Lesson' from *A Tropical Childhood and Other Poems* (Oxford University Press, 1961), reprinted by permission of Rogers, Coleridge & White; **p12 Dylan Thomas:** 'The Hunchback in the Park' from *Collected Poems 1934–1952* (J.M.Dent/Everyman's Library, 1977); **p15 Rudyard Kipling:** 'The Way through the Woods' from *Rewards and Fairies* (Macmillan, 1910); **p18 D.H. Lawrence:** 'Afternoon in School, The Last Lesson' from *Poems*, Selected and Introduced by Keith Sagar, Revised Edition (Penguin Poetry Library, 1986); **p30 James Bowen and Garry Jenkins:** from *A Street Cat Named Bob* (Hodder & Stoughton, 2012); **p33 Amy Pastan:** from *Gandhi* (Dorling Kindersley, 2006); **p36 Sally Gardner:** from *Tinder* (Orion Publishing Group, 2013); **p39 Nicola Klein:** Review of a production of Oliver! by the Cambridge Operatic Society with the Young Actors' Company from *Sardines Magazine* (2012), reprinted by permission of Sardines Magazine; **p42 Sara Smyth:** 'Half-term to be hit by wind and rain' from the *Daily Mail* (22 October, 2013), reprinted by permission of Solo Syndication; **p48 Michael Morpurgo:** from *Alone on a Wide Wide Sea* (HarperCollins, 2006); **p51 Leon Garfield:** from 'Shakespeare's Stories' (Gollancz, 1985); **p57 Elizabeth Gaskell:** from *Cranford* (1851); **p60 Adeline Yen Mah:** from *Watching the Tree* (HarperCollins, 2000); **p63 Charles Dickens:** from *Great Expectations* (1860–1); **p66 Robert Southey:** 'The Cataract of Lodore' (1820); **p75 Rachel Campbell-Johnston:** from *The Child's Elephant* (David Fickling Books, 2013), reprinted by permission of The Random House Group; **p78 Eva Ibbotson:** from *The Morning Gift* (Young Picador, 1993, 2007).

Every effort has been made to trace all copyright holders, but if any have been inadvertently overlooked the publishers will be pleased to make the necessary arrangements at the first opportunity.

Although every effort has been made to ensure that website addresses are correct at time of going to press, Galore Park cannot be held responsible for the content of any website mentioned in this book. It is sometimes possible to find a relocated web page by typing in the address of the home page for a website in the URL window of your browser.

Hachette UK's policy is to use papers that are natural, renewable and recyclable products and made from wood grown in sustainable forests. The logging and manufacturing processes are expected to conform to the environmental regulations of the country of origin.

Orders: please contact Bookpoint Ltd, 130 Milton Park, Abingdon, Oxon OX14 4SB. Telephone: +44 (0)1235 827827. Lines are open 9.00a.m.–5.00p.m., Monday to Saturday, with a 24-hour message answering service. Visit our website at www.galorepark.co.uk for details of other revision guides for Common Entrance, examination papers and Galore Park publications.

Published by Galore Park Publishing Ltd
An Hachette UK company
338 Euston Road, London, NW1 3BH
www.galorepark.co.uk

Text copyright © Susan Elkin Ltd 2014
The right of Susan Elkin to be identified as the author of this Work has been asserted by her in accordance with sections 77 and 78 of the Copyright, Designs and Patents Act 1988.

Impression number 10 9 8 7 6 5 4 3 2 1
2018 2017 2016 2015 2014

Typeset in India
Printed in Spain

A catalogue record for this title is available from the British Library.

ISBN: 978 1 471829 65 9

Contents

Contents

Introduction

If you can read with understanding it will help all your work in English – and, for that matter, in other, subjects too.

This workbook will help 9–11 year olds to improve their skills in:

- reading for meaning
- close reading
- deduction
- understanding implication and nuance
- appreciating how writers use language to gain their effects
- learning the meaning of unfamiliar words in context so that personal vocabulary grows
- writing accurate but detailed answers and responses to questions about reading.

This workbook consists of 25 comprehension passages with questions to practise on – at home with parents, in school, or for homework. They range widely across fiction, poetry and various sorts of non-fiction including memoir, biography, review, journalism and factual information.

Although this book is not linked to a particular examination syllabus, it will help users prepare for:

- Common Entrance 11+ in English
- 11+ entry English tests set by individual independent schools
- 11+ in English for selective state-funded schools in certain local authorities (such as Kent)
- National Curriculum Key Stage 2 SATS English tests
- pre-tests.

I hope too that this book will encourage you to read more. If you like what you read here, go the library and find the book the extract comes from so that you can read the rest of it.

Some suggested answers are supplied but these are simply for guidance and example. There are very few 'right' or 'wrong' answers in this sort of work. Many of the questions asked could be answered in different ways.

You can find the answers in a pull-out section in the middle of the book.

Susan Elkin, September 2014

Travels with Charley

John Steinbeck, a highly respected, award-winning American author who died in 1968, drove through most American states in a camper van with his dog in 1960. His book *Travels with Charley* was the result.

I had never been to Wisconsin, but all my life I had heard about it, had eaten its cheeses, some of them as good as any in the world. And I must have seen pictures. Everyone must have. Why then was I unprepared for the beauty of this region, for its variety of field and hill, forest, lake? I think now I must have considered it one big level cow pasture because of the state's enormous yield of milk products. I never saw a country that changed so rapidly, and because I had not expected it everything I saw brought a delight. I don't know how it is in other seasons, the summer may reek and rock with heat, the winters may groan with dismal cold, but when I saw it for the first and only time in early October, the air was rich with butter-colored sunlight, not fuzzy but crisp and clear so that every frost-gay tree was set off, the rising hills were not compounded, but alone and separate. There was a penetration of the light into solid substance so that I seemed to see into things, deep in, and I've seen that kind of light elsewhere only in Greece. I remembered now that I had been told Wisconsin is a lovely state, but the telling had not prepared me. It was a magic day. The land dripped with richness, the fat cows and pigs gleaming against green, and, in the smaller holdings, corn standing in little tents as corn should, and pumpkins all about.

I don't know whether or not Wisconsin has a cheese-tasting festival, but I who am a lover of cheese believe it should. Cheese was everywhere, cheese centers, cheese cooperatives, cheese stores and stands, perhaps even cheese ice cream. I can believe anything, since I saw a score of signs advertising Swiss Cheese Candy. Now I can't persuade anyone that it exists, that I did not make it up.

From *Travels with Charley* by John Steinbeck (1980)

Exercise ●

1 What is Wisconsin's main farming activity and product?

_____

_____

_____

_____

_____ (3)

2 List three words or phrases that indicate the author's positive reaction to Wisconsin.

_____

_____

_____ (1)

3 What do you learn about the climate of Wisconsin from this passage?

_____

_____

_____

_____

_____

_____

_____

_____

_____

_____ (5)

4 What does the author mean by

(a) 'corn standing in little tents as corn should'

_____

_____

_____

_____ (3)

(b) 'perhaps even cheese ice cream'?

_____

_____

_____

_____ (3)

5 What surprises the author about Wisconsin?

_____
_____
_____
_____
_____
_____
_____
_____ (4)

6 Summarise what you learn about the state of Wisconsin from this passage.

_____
_____
_____
_____
_____
_____
_____
_____
_____
_____
_____
_____ (6)

> Anything you quote – from a passage or poem of
> any sort – should be enclosed in inverted commas
> (sometimes called 'quotation marks').

The Lesson

Poet Edward Lucie-Smith was born in 1933. This poem looks back to his schooldays.

'Your father's gone,' my bald headmaster said.
His shiny dome and brown tobacco jar
Splintered at once in tears. It wasn't grief.
I cried for knowledge which was bitterer
Than any grief. For there and then I knew
That grief has uses – that a father dead
Could bind the bully's fist for a week or two;
And then I cried for shame, then for relief.

I was a month past ten when I heard this:
I still remember how the noise was stilled
In school-assembly when my grief came in.
Some goldfish in a bowl quietly sculled
Around their shining prison on its shelf.
They were indifferent. All the other eyes
Were turned towards me. Somewhere in myself
Pride, like a goldfish, flashed a sudden fin.

'The Lesson' by Edward Lucie-Smith (1961)

Exercise ●

1 How old is the narrator when his father dies?

_____ (1)

2 Who tells him the news and where?

_____

_____

_____

_____

_____

_____ (3)

3 (a) What is the narrator's first thought when he hears the news?

_____

_____

_____

_____

_____

_____ (3)

(b) Why does he feel shame?

_____

_____

_____

_____

_____ (3)

4 What does the poet mean by

(a) 'Splintered at once in tears'

_____

_____

_____

_____

_____ (2)

(b) 'when my grief came in'?

_____

_____

_____

_____

_____ (2)

5 What is the reaction of other pupils?

_____

_____

_____

_____

_____

_____

_____ (5)

6 Why does he mention the goldfish?

_____

_____

_____

_____

_____

_____

_____

_____

_____

_____

_____

_____ (6)

> When you answer questions about poetry, use your own words but weave short, even single-word, quotations from the poem into your sentences.

The Hunchback in the Park

Welsh poet Dylan Thomas died in 1953, aged only 39. He is
best known for the poetic radio drama *Under Milk Wood*. Here
Thomas thoughtfully observes a lonely, disabled man.

The hunchback in the park
A solitary mister
Propped between trees and water
From the opening of the garden lock
That lets the trees and water enter
Until the Sunday sombre bell at dark

Eating bread from a newspaper
Drinking water from the chained cup
That the children filled with gravel
In the fountain basin where I sailed my ship
Slept at night in a dog kennel
But nobody chained him up.

Like the park birds he came early
Like the water he sat down
And Mister they called Hey Mister
The truant boys from the town
Running when he had heard them clearly
On out of sound

Past the lake and rockery
Laughing when he shook his paper
Hunchback in mockery
Through the loud zoo of the willow groves

Dodging the park keeper
With his stick that picked up leaves.

And the old dog sleeper
Alone between nurses and swans
While the boys among willows
Made the tigers jump out of their eyes
To roar on the rockery stones
And the groves were blue with sailors

Made all day until bell time
A woman figure without fault
Straight as a young elm
Straight and tall from his crooked bones
That she might stand in the night
After the locks and chains

All night in the unmade park
After the railings and shrubberies
The birds the grass the trees the lake
And the wild boys innocent as strawberries
Had followed the hunchback
To his kennel in the dark.

From `The Hunchback in the Park´ by Dylan Thomas (1977)

Exercise •

1 What is unusual about the punctuation and arrangement of verses in this poem?

_____

_____

_____

_____ (3)

2 Describe the park in your own words.

_____

_____

_____

_____

_____

_____ (4)

3 What does the park keeper do?

_____

_____

_____ (2)

4 What do you learn about the hunchback from this poem?

_____

_____

_____

_____

_____

_____

_____

_____ (5)

5 What does the narrator imagine might happen in the park at dusk?

_____

_____

_____

_____ (3)

6 Describe the 'truant boys' in your own words and using quotations from the poem.

_____

_____

_____

_____

_____

_____

_____

_____

_____

_____

_____

_____

_____ (5)

7 Who is the woman in the penultimate verse?

_____

_____

_____

_____

_____

_____

_____

_____ (3)

The Way through the Woods

English poet Rudyard Kipling (1865–1936) also wrote *The Jungle Book* and the *Just So Stories*.

They shut the way through the woods
　　　Seventy years ago.
Weather and rain have undone it again
　　　And now you would never know
There was once a road through the woods
　　　Before they planted the trees

It is underneath the coppice and heath,
　　　And the thin anemones.
　　　Only the keeper sees
That, where the ring-dove broods,
　　　And the badgers roll at ease,
There was once a road through the woods.

Yet, if you enter the woods
　　　Of a summer evening late,
When the night-air cools on the trout-ringed pools
　　　Where the otter whistles his mate,
(They fear not men in the woods,
　　　Because they see so few)
You will hear the beat of the horse's feet
　　　And the swish of a skirt in the dew,
　　　Steadily cantering through
The misty solitudes,
　　　As though they perfectly knew
The old lost road through the woods....
But there is no road through the woods.

`The Way through the Woods´ by Rudyard Kipling (1910)

Exercise ●

1 (a) How long ago did the road through the woods close?

_____ (1)

(b) Can you think of any reason why that length of time is particularly significant?

_____

_____

_____

_____

_____

_____

_____ (4)

2 What has happened since to the place where the road was?

_____

_____

_____

_____

_____

_____

_____ (4)

3 Which details does the poet include to make it clear that very few human beings go into the woods?

_____

_____

_____

_____

_____

_____

_____

_____

_____ (5)

4 What does the poet imagine in the last verse?

_____

_____

_____

_____ (2)

5 Kipling uses the word 'woods' seven times and the phrase 'way/road through the woods' five times in this 25-line poem. What is the effect of this repetition?

_____

_____

_____

_____

_____

_____

_____

_____ (4)

6 Write a short paragraph commenting on anything else you particularly like or dislike about this poem. Include some short quotations.

_____

_____

_____

_____

_____

_____

_____

_____

_____ (5)

Afternoon in School, The Last Lesson

Before he became a famous novelist and poet, D.H. Lawrence (1885–1930) was, briefly, a teacher in Croydon.

When will the bell ring, and end this weariness?
How long have they tugged at the leash, and strained apart
My pack of unruly hounds: I cannot start
Them again on a quarry of knowledge they hate to hunt,
I can haul them and urge them no more.
No more can I endure to bear the brunt
Of the books that lie out on the desks: a full three score
Of several insults of blotted pages and scrawl
Of slovenly work that they have offered me.
I am sick, and tired more than any thrall
Upon the woodstacks working weariedly.

     And shall l take
The last dear fuel and heap it on my soul
Till I rouse my will like a fire to consume
Their dross of indifference, and burn the scroll
Of their insults in punishment? – I will not!

I will not waste myself to embers for them,
Not all for them shall the fires of my life be hot,
For myself a heap of ashes of weariness, till sleep
Shall have raked the embers clear: I will keep
Some of my strength for myself, for if I should sell
It all for them, I should hate them –
     – I will sit and wait for the bell.

`Afternoon in School, The Last Lesson´ by D.H. Lawrence (1986)

Exercise ●

1 Pick three words from the poem which clearly indicate that the narrator does not enjoy teaching.

_____

_____

_____ (1)

2 Give another word or phrase that means the same as

   (a) brunt

   _____ (1)

   (b) thrall

   _____ (1)

   (c) dross.

   _____ (1)

3 **(a)** What does he compare his pupils with in the second and third lines?

   _____

   _____ (2)

   (b) How does he further develop this idea in lines 3, 4 and 5?

   _____

   _____

   _____

   _____

   _____

   _____

   _____

   _____ (5)

4 What does the poet tell us about the pupils' exercise books?

   _____

   _____

   _____

   _____

   _____

   _____

   _____ (4)

5 What is his attitude to punishing them for their bad behaviour?

_____

_____

_____

_____

_____

_____

_____ (5)

6 How does the narrator feel overall?

_____

_____

_____

_____

_____

_____

_____

_____

_____

_____

_____ (5)

It often helps, when you're tackling a comprehension (other than in an exam of course), to discuss it with another pupil or an adult before you try to write your answers.

Captain Cook

Captain Cook is famous for being the first European to land in Australia. This passage is about his background.

It's a bitterly cold, icy winter's night in October 1728. Imagine a one-up, one-down, earth-floored cottage in the village of Marton which is now in North Yorkshire, near Whitby.

Hundreds of miles to the south in London, white-wigged, britches-clad George II has just become King and is strutting about elegantly enjoying the music of Mr Handel whose stuff is the Georgian equivalent of top of the pops.

But back in that rush-lit farm worker's cottage, Grace Cook doesn't at this moment care much who's king.

Miraculously, against all the odds of poor hygiene, inadequate diet, cramped conditions and non-existent obstetric care, Grace gives birth to a healthy son, named James after his father. He is destined to go a long way – in every sense.

James was sent to the village school where he learned to read and write. Later he worked in a shop on the coast where he fell in love with the sea and said: 'I'm determined to go to sea and seek my fortune.'

He asked a local family of trading bigwigs, the Walkers, for help. They were Quakers who admired James Cook's sober enthusiasm so they decided to give him a chance. Thus he learned the craft of seafaring by sailing in creaky timber cargo ships up and down the east coast of Britain, mostly carrying coal from the mines in the north east of England to London.

So James Cook had found his metier. He was rapidly promoted, passed some exams and sailed farther afield in Walkers' ships. 'I'd like to offer you the command of one of my ships,' Mr Walker told the 27-year-old James in 1755.

But that wasn't what this ambitious young man wanted. He had set his sights on even wider horizons so he volunteered for the Royal Navy. He shone there too – charting coastal waters, making scientific observations, serving in North America and taking part in action against the French during the Seven Years War.

Cook's big break came in 1768 when the Admiralty offered him the command of a Whitby-built ship, the *Endeavour*, with a mission to sail to Tahiti to make observations of Venus. It was the first of his three great voyages.

Cook was eventually killed by frenzied warriors as the result of ill-judged, high-handed colonialism against the king of Hawaii in 1779 – not quite the end his tearful, but joyful, mother might have envisaged for her son back in that humble cottage in 1728.

1 How old was James Cook when he died?

_____ (1)

2 Describe in your own words the cottage in which he was born.

_____

_____

_____

_____

_____ (4)

3 Why is it surprising to us in the twenty-first century that Grace gave birth to a healthy baby?

_____

_____

_____

_____

_____

_____

_____

_____ (5)

4 How did James Cook learn the craft of seafaring?

_____

_____

_____ (3)

5 What do you learn about James Cook's personality from this passage?

_____

_____

_____

_____

_____

_____

_____

_____

_____ (6)

6 Why does the writer mention the court of George II?

_____

_____

_____

_____

_____

_____

_____

_____

_____

_____ (6)

Use phrases such as 'I deduce that' or 'I conclude that' in your answers.

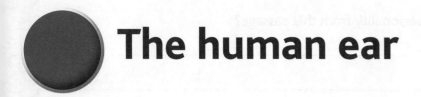

The human ear

This factual passage explains how the human ear works.

The bit we call the ear on the side of the head is just the trumpet or funnel which traps the sound. The works, which are what really matters, are out of sight.

The pinna – that's the fleshy trumpet – leads via the ear canal into two tiny but vital chambers: the middle ear and the inner ear. Think of it as a journey. Imagine you're a sound wave.

First you go along the waxy-walled ear canal. Then you meet the ear drum – a sensitive vibrating membrane called the tympanum which is stretched across the entrance to the middle ear. You – the sound wave – pass across and through it.

The next stage in your adventure is the crossing of the cavity of the middle ear. You do it via a mini bridge formed by the body's three smallest bones. They're actually called ossicles rather than bones to remind you how tiny they are. This pretty little trio are imaginatively shaped like a mallet, an anvil and a stirrup and they lead the way across the void to the oval window which is the gateway to the inner ear.

But before we penetrate the depths of the inner ear, stop being a sound wave for a minute and think about pressure. Know that feeling when you're in a deep tunnel or an aircraft and you don't adjust immediately to the changed pressure so your ears block? That's because the atmospheric pressure in the middle ear cavity needs changing. Yawning will do the trick. So will swallowing (one of the airline's boiled sweets if you're lucky, or your own mints if you're not) because of the handy little Eustachian tube which runs from one corner of the middle ear through to your airy throat.

To the inner ear. It's fluid filled and includes the cochlea and the semi-circular canals. The former looks like a coiled-up snail and it transmits the sound along its branch of the auditory nerve safely home into the brain where it gets sorted out and interpreted.

The semi-circular canals do a separate job in this diminutive, but busy, corner of the body. And they have their own hotline to the auditory nerve. There are three of them and each lies in a different plane across the other two. Together they control your balance. If they go wrong you fall over, get vertigo, feel dizzy or something worse. That's why a severe inner ear infection can affect balance.

Exercise ●

1 (a) What is the proper name for the part of the ear which is visible on the side of the head?

_____ (1)

(b) What is its function?

_____

_____ (2)

2 What are

(a) ossicles

_____ (1)

(b) tympanum

_____ (1)

(c) cochlea

_____ (1)

(d) vertigo?

_____ (1)

3 The ear, as a whole, has two quite separate purposes. What are they?

_____ (2)

4 Explain what the Eustachian tube does.

_____

_____

_____

_____

_____

_____

_____

_____ (6)

5 What is the brain's role in hearing?

_____

_____

_____

_____

_____

_____ (4)

6 What does the writer mean by 'this diminutive, but busy, corner of the body'?

_____

_____

_____

_____

_____

_____

_____

_____

_____

_____

_____

_____

_____

_____ (6)

It is best to read the passage at least twice before you
attempt to answer any questions.

Nurse Edith Cavell

This is a factual piece about Nurse Edith Cavell who died in the
First World War.

Near the entrance to the National Portrait Gallery on a traffic island in the middle
of Charing Cross Road in London stands a statue of a woman. She died on 17
October 1915. Her name was Edith Cavell and she was executed by firing squad by
the Germans in occupied Belgium, accused of hiding and helping British soldiers
to get home safely.

So just who was Edith Cavell and what did she really do? At first a governess,
Edith then looked after her invalid father, which convinced her that she had a
vocation for nursing. At the age of 30 she became a full-time nurse and worked in
England for ten years.

She was clearly an excellent nurse because in 1906 she was invited to start
a training school for nurses in Brussels. She accepted the job and founded the
Belgian nursing service. Belgium needed a professional nursing service because
hitherto all nurses had been nuns who, caring as they usually were, had no medical
training and little skill.

So Edith trained Belgian women to nurse and by 1914 she had created a small
but growing body of competent nurses. Then war broke out and within three weeks
the Germans had invaded Belgium and occupied it.

The Germans offered to take her out of Belgium to safety in Holland which
wasn't involved in the war. But Edith refused to go. Instead she and her nurses
remained where they were and nursed the casualties of all warring nations,
including Germans.

She also helped soldiers from Britain and its allies to escape and that was what
led to her being arrested, court-martialled and shot at dawn.

Edith immediately became world famous. There was horror in many countries
that a woman should have been treated like this and people were even more
outraged because she was a nurse who had been trying to help people.

Edith was a deeply committed Christian and she died bravely, telling the British
chaplain the night before her execution that, as a nurse, she'd seen so much death
that she wasn't frightened of it.

So think of her if you pass her statue – or Cavell Road or Cavell Street in London,
or Cavell Mountain in Canada or any of the many other places named after her. I
suspect, though, that she would much rather be remembered for the excellent work
she did in developing professional training for nurses than as a 'heroine' shot by the
Germans.

1 Name three things that commemorate Edith Cavell in London today.

_____

_____

_____ (3)

2 What inspired her to take up nursing?

_____

_____ (2)

3 How and when did Edith Cavell die?

_____

_____ (2)

4 Apart from being executed by the Germans, what would she probably have liked to be remembered for?

_____

_____

_____

_____

_____ (4)

5 What was her attitude to nursing people after the First World War broke out?

_____

_____

_____

_____

_____

_____ (4)

6 What was her 'crime' against the Germans?

_____

_____

_____

_____

_____

_____

_____ (4)

7 Explain in your own words why Edith Cavell 'immediately became world famous'.

_____

_____

_____

_____

_____

_____

_____

_____

_____

_____

_____

_____

_____ (6)

When you read a passage use a highlighter pen or a
pencil to mark words, phrases, and so on, which seem
particularly important.

A Street Cat Named Bob

In *A Street Cat Named Bob* James Bowen, a former drug addict now working as a busker, describes his friendship with Bob, a cat who teams up with him.

As darkness was beginning to descend, one middle-aged lady stopped for a chat.

'How long have you had him?' she asked, bending down to stroke Bob.

'Oh, only a few weeks,' I said. 'We sort of found each other.'

'Found each other? Sounds interesting.'

At first I was a bit suspicious. I wondered whether she was some kind of animal welfare person and might tell me I had no right to keep him or something. But she turned out simply to be a real cat lover.

She smiled as I explained the story of how we'd met and how I'd spent a fortnight nursing him back to health.

'I had a ginger tom very much like this one a few years ago,' she said, looking a bit emotional. For a moment I thought she was going to burst into tears. 'You are lucky to have found him. They are just the best companions, they are so quiet and docile. You've found yourself a real friend there,' she said.

'I think you are right,' I smiled.

She placed a fiver into the guitar case before leaving.

He was definitely a lady puller, I realised. I estimated that something like 70 per cent of the people who had stopped so far had been females.

After just over an hour, I had as much as what I'd normally make in a good day, just over twenty pounds.

This is brilliant, I thought to myself.

But something inside me was saying that I shouldn't call it quits, that I should carry on for tonight.

The truth was that I was still torn about Bob. Despite the gut feeling I had that this cat and I were somehow destined to be together, a large part of me still figured that he'd eventually go off and make his own way. It was only logical. He'd wandered into my life and he was going to wander back out again at some point. This couldn't carry on. So as the passers-by continued to slow down and make a fuss of him, I figured I might as well make the most of it. Make hay while the sun shines and all that.

'If he wants to come out and have fun with me, that's great,' I said to myself. 'And if I'm making a bit of cash as well, then that's great too.'

From *A Street cat Named Bob* by James Bowen (2012)

Exercise ●

1 What sort of cat is Bob?

_____ (1)

2 What instrument do you deduce that the narrator plays?

_____

_____ (1)

3 What problem did the narrator face when he first met Bob?

_____

_____

_____

_____ (3)

4 Why is the narrator initially wary of the lady and what changes his mind?

_____

_____

_____

_____

_____

_____

_____

_____

_____ (6)

5 What financial advantage is Bob bringing the narrator?

_____

_____

_____

_____

_____

_____

_____

_____ (6)

6 What does the narrator expect to happen in the future and how does that affect his decisions now?

_____

_____

_____

_____

_____

_____

_____

_____

_____

_____

_____ (8)

There are very few absolute right and wrong answers in English comprehension work. Your opinion is as 'right' as anyone else's as long as you can support what you say by referring to the passage you are working on.

Gandhi

Mohandas Gandhi worked peacefully but determinedly all his life for the independence of India (from Britain) and for the equality of all its people. In this passage Amy Pastan describes Gandhi's violent death in 1948, just as his life-long hopes had begun to come true.

On 30 January, Gandhi was still weak from his fast, but he hurried to his evening prayer meeting; he hated to be late. Supported on each side by his grandnieces Manubehn and Abhabehn, he entered the large garden at Birla House where an expectant crowd awaited him. Gandhi raised his hands, palms clasped together to greet his supporters. Many tried to come forward to touch the feet of the man they worshipped, but one man forced himself past the others. As he kneeled before the Mahatma, he aimed a semi-automatic pistol at Gandhi's heart and pulled the trigger. Uttering '*He Ram*' ('Oh God'), Gandhi fell back. His khadi was stained with blood, he slumped to the ground, and his heart stopped beating. His face was at peace.

Gandhi's assassin was caught after a brief struggle. His name was Nathuram Godse. Godse was a member of a Hindu extremist group that felt betrayed by Gandhi because he showed support to Muslims. Others had helped Godse plan the Mahatma's murder. Godse and one of his fellow co-conspirators were later tried, convicted, and executed for the crime.

For Jawaharlal Nehru, who had now become prime minister of India, Gandhi had been almost a father. His voice breaking with emotion, he addressed his new and troubled nation on the radio after he learned the sad news of the Mahatma's death:

'The light has gone out of our lives and there is darkness everywhere and I do not quite know what to tell you and how to say it. Our beloved leader, Bapu as we called him, the father of our nation, is no more ... The light has gone out, I said, and yet I was wrong. For the light that shone in this country was no ordinary light. The light that has illumined this country for these many years, and the world will see it and it will give solace to innumerable hearts. For that light represented the living truth, and the eternal man was with us with his eternal truth reminding us of the right path, drawing us from error, taking this ancient country to freedom ...'

From an account by Amy Pastan in *Gandhi* published by Dorling Kindersley (2006)

1 Where was Gandhi going on the evening of his assassination?

_____

_____

_____

_____

_____

_____ (3)

2 What help did he need and why?

_____

_____

_____

_____ (3)

3 Gandhi's given name was Mohandas.

   (a) What other name or title, meaning a respected wise man or sage, was he often known by?

_____ (1)

   (b) What other name meaning leader was he often addressed as?

_____ (1)

4 How exactly was he killed?

_____

_____

_____

_____

_____

_____

_____

_____ (5)

5 Why was he killed?

_____

_____

_____

_____ (4)

6 How were the conspirators punished?

_____

_____

_____

_____ (2)

7 What did Nehru mean by 'that light represented the living truth'?

_____

_____

_____

_____

_____

_____

_____

_____

_____

_____

_____

_____ (6)

Take care to spell correctly any proper nouns (such as names) from the passage that you use in your answers.

Tinder

This is the opening of Sally Gardner's 2013 novel *Tinder,* which is set in the seventeenth century.

Once in a time of war, when I was a soldier in the Imperial Army, I saw Death walking. He wore upon his skull a withered crown of white bone twisted with green hawthorn. His skeleton was shrouded with a tattered cloak of gold and in his wake stood the ghosts of my comrades newly plucked, half-lived, from life. Many I knew by name.

It was on the second day of November 1642, in the midst of the battle of Breitenfeld, when our regiment had been trapped in the great forest, caught between the criss-cross of trees and the oncoming guns of the enemy. Cannon blast sent fire into the woods and in the smoke I couldn't tell which way the fight ran. In the distance, the sound of horses, bridles and harnesses. I'd been in battle since dawn. Like many of my comrades I'd fought for all I was worth, though I knew ours was a hopeless cause. About me lay the dead and the dying, their blood – our blood – made the carpet of leaves more crimson than autumn had intended.

That was when I saw Death.

He seemed neither surprised nor impressed by the number of souls he had gathered that day. He simply asked me if I was with him.

I looked upon the ghostly army and wondered if it wouldn't be best to follow for, in truth, I'd had enough of war, had seen too much of man's inhumane heart.

'I wait for no one,' said Death.

'You've feasted well today,' I said. 'What difference would my soul make?'

It was then that Death and his ghostly army vanished. In their place a thick mist rose and through the mist a horseman came charging, sword in hand. Without another thought, I turned and ran. I ran until every muscle, every sinew strained to the edge of breaking. I ran until I had no breath left, my boots giving out before my legs fell away beneath me. I ran until the ground and I became one. I lay unable to move, only stare at the canopy of leaves all golden, all falling in spirals of colour. I listened for the sound of hooves, for the howl of a wolf, for the growl of a bear. I knew well that if the battle did not kill me then the forest would, for the smell of blood brings beasts out to feed. I lay injured, a bullet in my side, a sword wound in my shoulder, watching night creep through the trees. Maybe I should have gone with Death when he offered me his bony finger.

From *Tinder* by Sally Gardner (2013)

Exercise •••••••••••••••••••••••••••••••••

1 List the weapons and resources used in this battle.

_____

_____

_____

_____ (1)

2 What does the figure of Death look like?

_____

_____

_____

_____ (2)

3 Quote two sentences which show that the narrator is close to losing the will to live.

_____

_____

_____

_____

_____ (4)

4 What accompanies Death and why is this significant?

_____

_____

_____

_____

_____

_____ (5)

5 Explain in your own words what the narrator really means by seeing Death.

_____

_____

_____

_____

_____

_____

_____

_____ (5)

6 For the narrator's side it was 'a hopeless cause'. Why?

_____

_____

_____

_____

_____

_____ (4)

7 How is the narrator injured and where does he go?

_____

_____

_____

_____

_____ (4)

> Think of the passage as being like a lemon from which you have to squeeze as much juice as possible. That means close attention to every word you read and 'juicy' detailed answers.

Oliver!

This is a review by Nicola Klein of a production of *Oliver!* in 2012 by the Cambridge Operatic Society with the Young Actors' Company, directed by Leigh Macdonald. It was published in the online version of *Sardines* magazine.

One of the big advantages of *Oliver!* for a non-professional company is that it is studded with small roles each of which is a gem. The strong principals who play these roles can then be used as chorus for the rest of the show which makes, when you have as much talent to call on as Cambridge Operatic Society does, for a very strong chorus. And that adds a lot to the success of the production.

Another big advantage, of course, is Lionel Bart's iconic, show-stopping numbers, which spill out one after another. Familiar they may be but the quality and variety is such that they never seem to pall. No wonder this show played to packed houses for eight performances – fully sold out except for a few seats at the first performance. Parents and friends of the cast, including all those children, school parties and the general public flocked into the Cambridge Arts Theatre.

Scott Riley, slimy, lithe and long haired with nasal speaking voice, mobile fingers – and a fine singer with perfect intonation and timing – is as good a Fagin as I've ever seen. And yes, I did see Ron Moody do it in a 1980s revival. Other outstanding performances include William Hale as a sardonic Mr Sowerberry, Mandy Jeffery as self-interested Widow Corney, Anna Murgatroyd (very accomplished and rather underused) as Mrs Bedwin and Eileen Donnelly as a deliciously passionate Nancy. Alan Hay is a suitably gravelly Bill Sykes and young Zebb Dempster, who finds every possible drop of unpleasantness in Noah Claypole, is one to watch out for in future CaOS shows.

And so to the children. In the performance which I saw Josh Bailey (alternating with Harry Gee) gave us a spirited Dodger although his spoken words aren't always audible. He has masses of stage presence though and sings and dances with well-controlled ebullience. Alex Hearne-Potton (alternating with Alexander Boyd-Bench) is gentle and charming as Oliver which goes some way to offsetting the intonation problems in his singing. The children's chorus – girls as well as boys in this show – is lively, tuneful and splendidly choreographed by Danielle Phillips who knows exactly how to keep them moving in a visually interesting way. The scenes in the orphanage and in Fagin's den are very professional, although the children strain for some of the higher notes.

Rarely have I heard a production of *Oliver!* which so clearly highlights the fine orchestration as adeptly as this version for eleven-piece band does, under the baton of Lucas Elkin in the pit. We hear lots of bassoon work, some neat trombone interjection, fine support from piano and Fagin's famous Klesmer number 'I'm reviewing the situation' with beautifully controlled accompanying solo violin – slightly different for each verse – makes for a lovely bit of musical theatre.

© Nicola Klein 2012

Exercise ●

1 Explain the meaning of

(a) iconic

_____ (1)

(b) sardonic

_____ (1)

(c) ebullience

_____ (1)

(d) intonation

_____ (1)

2 (a) Who wrote *Oliver!*?

_____ (1)

(b) Who played Fagin when the show was new and again in the 1980s?

_____ (1)

3 Why does the reviewer think that *Oliver!* is a good choice of show for an amateur company?

_____

_____

_____

_____ (2)

4 What do you learn from this review about

(a) Scott Riley

_____

_____

_____

_____

_____

_____ (2)

Answers

Travels with Charley (page 6)

1 Dairy farming for the production of cheese is the main farming activity in Wisconsin. (It also has pigs and it grows corn and pumpkins.) Steinbeck sees cheese shops and references to other cheese businesses. He is also amused by the numerous signs advertising Swiss Cheese Candy.

2 Possibilities include: 'beauty', 'delight', 'rich', 'lovely'

3 The author suspects that it has hot summers which 'reek and rot' and cold winters, although he can't be sure because he has no direct experience of it in those seasons. In October, when he visits, there is mellow ('buttercolored') sunshine and only slight frosts whose ice shines prettily in the 'frost-gay' trees.

4 (a) The corn has been cut and is piled across the field in miniature stacks, like little pyramids, in the traditional way.

  (b) He is joking that because the people of Wisconsin present their cheese in so many different ways that maybe they even use it as an ice cream flavour.

5 He doesn't expect it to be as beautiful as it is. He is impressed by the changing scenery which includes fields, hills, forests and lakes. He enjoys the autumn sunlight and the clear views of the hills which it affords. He had been told that Wisconsin is attractive, but on this, his first visit, he is still surprised to find that that it 'dripped with richness'.

6 The state is very green and fertile which is why it can support an extensive dairy industry including many cheese-producing companies. Its high quality cheese is widely sent elsewhere in America – Steinbeck has often eaten and admired it. It includes a lot of pasture for the cattle, along with fields where crops such as corn and pumpkins are grown. In October the sunny autumn light across the hills, forests and fields is lovely and reminds the author of Greece.

The Lesson (page 9)

1 He is just ten.

2 He is told by his headmaster that his father has died. Presumably the two of them are in the headmaster's study because the boy remembers the brown tobacco jar so this isn't a classroom. It's a more personal room.

3 (a) He thinks that the bullies – who have evidently been making him very unhappy and hurting him – will leave him alone for a bit. He knows that a 'father dead/Could bind the bully's fist for a week or two'.

  (b) He feels ashamed because he knows that he should be feeling grief for his father not relief that something has happened to save him, even temporarily, from the bullies.

4 (a) His eyes filling with tears blurred his vision so that the two things he remembers looking at most clearly – the bald head and the tobacco jar – remain in his memory as a broken image.

  (b) In assembly, later, when he takes in the full reality of what has happened the real grief starts or

'comes in' and he starts to feel his loss. It is a delayed reaction.

5 They look at him with 'shining eyes'. It is as if, suddenly, they admire him, perhaps envying him for being the centre of attention because something momentous has happened to him. They are – probably temporarily – in awe of him. And the narrator understands all this because, one infers, he has seen it happen to others.

6 The goldfish offer a stark comparison to the narrator's mixed feelings. They are trapped in their 'shining prison' and 'indifferent' to anything outside their bowl. For them it is life as usual and that helps to highlight the intensity of the boy's feelings. When, in the last line of the poem he, ashamedly, feels a flash of pride it reminds him of the fin of the goldfish operating completely outside the grief that he's feeling.

The Hunchback in the Park (page 12)

1 The poem is laid out in seven six-line verses but contains only three full stops. The meaning therefore runs across the verse endings and beginnings – which is known technically as enjambment. It means you have to read the first two verses as one statement, the second two as another and the last three verses as the concluding thought, rather than stopping at line or verse endings.

2 The park has trees including willows. There is a rockery. It includes areas of bushy vegetation or shrubberies. There is an ornamental lake with swans. One of its features is a fountain with a drinking cup on a chain. The whole area is surrounded by perimeter railings and there are lockable gates.

3 He patrols the park while clearing up leaves with a spiked stick. He is, we infer, also a figure of authority because the truant boys dodge him.

4 The hunchbacked man is alone in the park all day every day sitting between the trees and the lake. He eats bread wrapped in newspaper and drinks water from the fountain. The narrator – and the children and passers-by – do not know where he goes at night after the park is closed and locked so the poet imagines that he sleeps in a kennel like a dog. The poet compares the sleepy man with an 'old dog sleeper'.

5 A bell rings ('sombre bell at dark' and 'bell time') to indicate that everyone must leave. Everything disappears and goes somewhere else as the park becomes 'unmade' like a bed.

6 The truant boys should be at school but are not. Instead they spend their days in the park taunting the hunchback man. They make 'the tigers jump out of their eyes' and 'roar' as they try to frighten him. They shout 'Hey Mister' and run away when he looks up. After the park has closed for the night the narrator imagines the truant boys following the man to his 'kennel in the dark'.

7 She is a sort of ghost or fantasy standing 'Straight and tall' in contrast to the man with his curved back. The

poet imagines her occupying the park, created from the 'crooked bones' of the disabled man, at night as another side of the hunchback's personality.

The Way through the Woods (page 15)

1 (a) The road was closed seventy years ago.
   (b) It means that almost nobody can actually remember the road. You would need to be over 75 to recall it. Therefore the narrator and local people only know about the way or road because they have been told about it. That gives it an air of mystery because, in a sense, it is just a story passed on and may not be completely true.

2 It has grown over and trees have been planted – and repeatedly cut back to harvest thin branches (coppiced) over the years. There are flowers such as anemones at ground level. The obliteration of the road has been furthered by wind and rain ('weather') which will have made things grow and blown trees down or caused branches to fall.

3 Kipling stresses the quiet and the undisturbed wildlife. There is a ring-dove nesting in the trees and badgers play fearlessly where the road once was. There are ponds with trout and otters which you can see and hear late on a still summer evening as dusk falls and the temperature begins to drop. These creatures 'fear not men in the woods,/Because they see so few'.

4 He imagines the people from an earlier era who would once have used the old road, with the sound of horses' hooves, and long skirts rustling. For him, at dusk, on a summer evening they seem almost physically present.

5 The repetition seems like a mysterious recurring echo. It helps to suggest that the road itself is a sort of ghost which haunts the wood, mostly unseen, but occasionally imagined. It makes the poem feel like a wistful song. The very word 'woods' with its gentle consonant at the beginning, short vowel and hissing ending is soft in sound which adds to the atmosphere.

6 Pupils could use this opportunity to write about Kipling's use of rhyme, short lines, alliteration – repeated sounds or letters at the beginnings of words – or the inclusion of the keeper, among other possibilities.

Afternoon in School, The Last Lesson (page 18)

1 Possibilities include: weariness, unruly, haul, endure, brunt, sick, tired, weariedly, waste, hate

2 (a) burden or impact
   (b) slavery
   (c) rubbish, trash, worthlessness

3 (a) He compares them with hunting dogs or 'unruly hounds' tugging away from him on their leads.
   (b) He then likens the knowledge they ought to be searching for with the fox or deer which hounds would hunt – the quarry or prey. As the master of the hounds, so to speak, he cannot get them started on hunting knowledge – the 'quarry' – because they hate it. He is too weary and disillusioned to drag them into action or spur them on any more.

4 There are 60 (three score) exercise books lying on the children's desks. He says their handwriting is poor

('scrawl'), and the work, which is covered in careless inkblots, is of a low standard and badly done or 'slovenly'. There is, in short, no commitment to the work, which the pupils don't seem to care about any more than the teacher does.

5 He isn't going to bother to punish them because that would require anger or passion ('my will like a fire') in order to shake the pupils out of their apathy and he can't be bothered. 'I will not' he says, because he regards it as a waste. Instead he will leave them in their 'dross of indifference'.

6 He is exhausted by the strain of failing to teach well. He says 'I am sick, and tired'. He uses the word 'weariness' twice and 'weariedly' once. So instead of rousing himself to any effort ('embers for them') he decides to 'keep/Some of my strength for myself'. That is why he is simply waiting for the end-of-lesson bell to end his torment.

Captain Cook (page 21)

1 James Cook was 50 or 51 when he died (born 1728 and died 1779).

2 The cottage, built for a farm worker, is very small and humble. It has only one room on each of two floors and there are no floorboards – just the earth underfoot as you would have in a tent. At night the only lighting comes from lit rushes – there aren't even any wax candles.

3 There is no proper hygiene (such as running water or modern disinfectants). The cottage is very crowded ('cramped') which would have made it even less hygienic. There was no modern medical understanding or service ('non-existent obstetric care'). Grace and her children would not have had access to the range of healthy foods we can buy today – or even enough to eat at all. The writer refers to their 'inadequate diet'.

4 He learned how to manage ships by sailing the east coast of England in cargo ships. He also took some formal qualifications and was offered promotion by his bosses, the Walker family.

5 He was very determined, ambitious and hardworking. He trained for a long time on Walkers' ships before choosing the Royal Navy as a way of widening his experience, which – as it turned out – included service across the Atlantic and in a war. He was also, we infer, bossy and blinkered – or became so as he prospered. It was 'high-handed colonialism' or inappropriately trying to impose his ways (and the ways of Britain) on native people which led to his death at the hand of angry warriors in Hawaii.

6 The court of George II is mentioned for contrast. The author wants to make clear the difference between the colourful, glamorous, music-loving royal court in London, and first the squalor of an ordinary family's home in the north of England, and second James Cook's life spent almost always away from Britain on ships. It is also a way of putting James Cook's story into historical context. Many people have an image of the royal court from historical films, and so on. This is a way of telling them about another aspect of life at the same point in history.

   English Workbook: Reading and Comprehension Age 9–11 published by Galore Park

The human ear (page 24)

1 (a) pinna
   (b) It traps the sound like a trumpet or funnel and angles it into the rest of the ear.
2 (a) tiny bones
   (b) ear drum
   (c) a device which looks like a curled up snail and carries the sound to the auditory nerve
   (d) loss of balance
3 hearing and balance
4 The Eustachian tube runs from the back of the throat to the middle ear. Its job is to bring in extra air when necessary to regularise the pressure in the middle ear. This can be affected by the pressure around the hearer if he or she is, for example, in an aircraft at height. When the ears feel blocked under these circumstances you need to swallow or yawn to bring in air via the Eustachian tube, which usually clears the problem.
5 The brain receives messages via the auditory nerve which has picked up the sound waves via the pinna, middle and inner ear. The brain then sorts out these messages and interprets them so that the hearer knows what he or she has heard.
6 She means that the spaces inside the ear are very small. The three little bones which carry the sound across the middle ear are, for example, the smallest in the human body. But there is a lot going on here so it is 'busy'. Sound waves travel though all three compartments (outer, middle and inner) and are elaborately processed before they reach the auditory nerve and the brain. At the same time the semi-circular canals have their own complex job to do in controlling balance.

Nurse Edith Cavell (page 27)

1 Cavell Road, Cavell Street and a statue in Charing Cross Road
2 She looked after her ailing father and realised that she had a talent for caring for sick people.
3 She was executed – shot at dawn by a German firing squad on 17 October 1915.
4 She would probably have liked to be remembered for being a nurse who trained other nurses and, in particular, for founding the first professional nursing service in Belgium which, before 1906 when Nurse Cavell went to Brussels, had relied solely on untrained nuns.
5 She saw nursing, and training nurses, as her vocation in any situation so when the war started in 1914 and there were many wounded men she refused the German offer to take her to a place of safety. Instead Nurse Cavell and her nurses cared for any injured solder, regardless of his nationality.
6 She hid some British soldiers and helped them to escape back to Britain. When the Germans discovered her part in this they put her on trial and found her guilty – which of course in their eyes she was.
7 People of all nations across the world were horrified and shocked that the Germans should have executed a woman. Women didn't fight then and were regarded as the 'gentler sex'. In Edith Cavell's case it seemed even more outrageous as she was engaged in nursing wounded men irrespective of which side they were on.

A Street Cat Named Bob (page 30)

1 He is male and ginger ('a ginger tom').
2 I think the narrator is playing a guitar (he is collecting money in his guitar case).
3 Bob was ill – the narrator had to spend 'a fortnight nursing him back to health'.
4 She seems rather too interested in Bob and the narrator is afraid she works for an animal welfare organisation and is about to accuse him of cruelty to his cat. Then, when she tells him about her own cat, he realises she is just a fellow cat lover.
5 The cat is attracting people to stop and listen to the narrator's music and he is therefore making more money than he usually does. On a good day, without the cat, he might collect £20. On this occasion with Bob he makes that, including the single £5 donation from the cat-loving lady, in just an hour.
6 He thinks that because Bob is a stray cat – and cats tend to make their own decisions about whom to spend their life with – that their partnership will be temporary. 'He'd wandered into my life and was going to wander back out again at some point.' He therefore decides, on the day he's describing, to continue busking on his pitch for longer than usual in order to make the most of the Bob effect while it lasts.

Gandhi (page 33)

1 He was going to Hindu evening prayers, passing on the way through the extensive gardens at Birla House where large numbers of people were waiting for him and keen to be near him.
2 Gandhi had been fasting and was weak from lack of food. He was therefore being helped by his two grandnieces, one either side ensuring that he didn't fall over.
3 (a) Mahatma
   (b) Bapu
4 Nathuram Godse pushed his way to the front of the crowd and knelt down as if he were respecting the great man. Then he shot Gandhi accurately through the heart with a pistol. Gandhi died instantly and probably without pain because his face looked very relaxed.
5 Godse and other men who helped plan the assassination were Hindus with very strict views. They disapproved of the way in which Gandhi had supported Muslims as well as Hindus.
6 The assassin and one of the men who worked with him were executed.
7 In shock and shaking with emotion, prime minister Jawaharlal Nehru described Gandhi in language usually reserved for religious leaders such as Jesus Christ. He meant that Gandhi's work had changed the world for ever and that everything he did would live on like a permanent light shining on prejudice and injustice. In a sense, he implied, Gandhi hadn't died at all because nothing could kill the change in attitude that he had brought about.

Tinder (page 36)

1 guns, cannon, swords, horses
2 It is a skeleton wearing a ragged gold cloak. On its head is a crown made of bone woven with the soft twigs

of fresh hawthorn. It has bony fingers with which it beckons people.

3 'I looked upon the ghostly army and wondered if it wouldn't be best to follow for, in truth, I'd had enough of war, had seen too much of man's inhuman heart' and 'Maybe I should have gone with Death when he offered me his bony finger.'

4 Death is surrounded by a ghostly army of young ('half-lived') people he has summoned to join him. Many of these were people who had been fighting with the narrator and he knows them by name. The significance is that these people are all recently dead. Death has gathered them up on the battlefield.

5 He means the battlefield he is on is a very dangerous place. People are dying around him and, injured, he comes close to death himself. So, in his pain, he imagines Death as a sinister figure who quietly haunts the battleground inviting souls to join him. The narrator resists Death with the question 'What difference would my soul make?' so Death and his ghostly army then disappear and the narrator lives on.

6 The regiment he belongs to is trapped in the forest with trees behind them and enemy guns coming towards them. Cannon have been fired into the wood causing smoke and confusion. In this long battle, which has been going on since dawn (and it is now dusk), the weary narrator can no longer be sure who is on which side. Many men have been killed and others are bleeding to death.

7 He has a bullet wound in his side and a sword wound in his shoulder. Somehow he finds the strength to run from an armed lone horseman into the woods where the rider cannot follow. There he rests briefly but knows he must not stay on the ground for long because wild animals such as bears and wolves pose a risk too, especially if they scent blood.

Oliver! (page 39)

1 (a) Having very special significance in the consciousness of many people perhaps because something is very well known, much loved and long lasting. An icon was, originally, a religious symbol and has come also to mean a label for a computer shortcut.
  (b) scornful or mocking
  (c) energetic excitement
  (d) pitching musical notes accurately

2 (a) Lionel Bart
  (b) Ron Moody

3 It has many strong well-known tunes and set sequences with a lot of characters. So, if you have a big cast to work with, there is plenty of enjoyable material for a large number of people to take part in.

4 (a) Scott Riley plays Fagin. He is thin and has, for the show at least, long hair. His fingers are very nimble and he uses them to act with. He sings well and in tune, using a voice which sounds as if it comes more from his nose than his chest. His dramatic timing marks him out as a good actor and the reviewer thinks he is as good as Ron Moody.
  (b) Anna Murgatroyd plays Mrs Bedwin. She is, in the view of the writer, a fine performer and should have been given a larger part.

5 (a) The writer is fairly impressed by Josh Bailey as the Dodger because he brings plenty of personality to his role and dances and sings with flair. Alex Hearne-Potton is appropriately sweet as Oliver. The movement work of the girls and boys in the chorus is excellent and the writer commends choreographer Danielle Phillips. On the whole, the chorus singing goes well too.
  (b) On the downside, the reviewer finds that Scott Bailey's spoken words cannot always be heard, that Alex Hearne-Potton does not always sing in tune and that the children in the chorus sometimes have difficulty reaching the high notes.

6 The accompanying orchestra consists of eleven players conducted by Lucas Elkin. The reviewer liked the detailed way in which individual instruments could be heard at different moments. She mentions, for example, hearing solo snippets from bassoon, trombone, piano and violin all making effective contributions. This takes careful control and the *Oliver!* band is good at it.

Wind and rain (page 42)

1 The areas likely to experience flooding are in the west of the country: south-western England and parts of the midlands, Wales and possibly parts of Scotland.

2 By elimination, the areas likely to avoid the worst weather are: London and south east England, and eastern England.

3 It is half term so there is an (unstated) assumption that families might be wanting to go on holiday or to enjoy days out.

4 (a) watchful, careful or alert
  (b) dangerous or risky

5 'unsettled', 'mobile'

6 Very variable conditions, including a lot of intermittent rain and persistent high winds, will bring a risk of flooding to many places in Scotland, Wales and the west of England during the next week or so.

7 (a) She quotes Chris Burton of MeteoGroup and an unnamed spokesman from Natural Resources Wales.
  (b) The quotations allow her to add more detail such as the risk of streams and ditches being unable to cope with unusually heavy rain and the rainfall statistic about Boscombe Down. These have the effect of making the piece seem more truthful because she seems to be supporting her statements with evidence through these speakers. The quotations also add variety to the way her article is expressed because the reader 'hears' two more voices as well as the journalist's. In fact the last three paragraphs are not essential to the main message of the piece and had they been omitted the reader would still have been given all the main facts.

Please Miss We're Boys (page 45)

1 He lives not far from the school in a rented flat in a block in Tidemill Road.

2 (a) diligent
  (b) laudable

(c) transpired

(d) condoned

3 The narrator is describing a situation from the past. It was long before the invention of internet banking and the easy transfer of money between accounts. And the members of the Paradise family were, the writer assumes, paid weekly in cash and probably didn't have a bank account so cheques weren't available to them either.

4 They are a Jamaican couple. They have a family of at least three boys, all of whom are either at school or working. Mr and Mrs Paradise, who are committed and fervent Christians, both go to work, probably in quite menial jobs as we are told that all the members of the family are paid their wages weekly in cash. They are sensible, likeable people who 'valued education' and by inference want the best for their children. But it is alien to their culture to get into any sort of debt. Therefore they have a strong commitment to paying the rent promptly every week. So, presumably reluctantly, they keep Bartholomew at home on Monday mornings to hand over the money.

5 Bartholomew is cheerful (smiles a lot) and polite. He is intelligent – 'plenty of sensible things to say in class discussions' and he never gets behind with his work, despite missing one morning a week of lessons. He is also honest. He tells the narrator the truth when she challenges him about his absences.

6 (a) She has grown up in a completely different social class and culture. Never before has she encountered anyone who has to stay in to pay weekly rent in her own 'family or social circle' or amongst the people she attended grammar school with. So Bartholomew's situation seems very strange to her.

(b) She deals with it with tact and wisdom. Although Mr and Mrs Paradise are breaking the law by keeping their son at home, the narrator and the Education Welfare Officer accept that if Bartholomew isn't falling behind with his work and, given that it's a good thing that his parents are so determined to pay their rent, the most appropriate reaction is to go along with it ('turned a blind eye') without saying so openly.

Alone on a Wide Wide Sea (page 48)

1 (a) The journey lasts about five or six days.

(b) As they ride on its back Big Black Jack is presumably a horse big enough to carry both boys.

2 (a) anger, violence or fear

(b) wondered

(c) quiet or keeping thoughts to oneself

(d) attacked (in play here) by surprise

3 They say very little but make it clear that they care about the two British boys and do not want to hurt them. Presumably because the boys are so different from them, the adult aboriginals stare at them a lot. They generously give the boys plenty to eat and drink – water, fruit and, once, roast meat. The narrator is aware that they don't wish to be too close or chatty and there is, anyway, no common language to talk in. By inference they don't understand, for example, when Marty tries to ask them where the group is going.

4 The children play and communicate with their 'visitors' in a very natural way. They clearly find them funny and there's a lot of laughter. Games they all play together – which don't need language – include stone skimming, stick throwing, some form of chasing ('ambushed one another') and giving the youngest ones rides on the horse.

5 They thought that perhaps the tribe had no specific intentions and that it had merely absorbed them to be a permanent part of the group alongside their own children. They also speculated that perhaps the tribe simply couldn't decide what do with them. Or, they thought, that one morning they might simply discover that the tribe had moved on without them.

6 After travelling for nearly a week the two boys are left somewhere – which was presumably the tribal people's intention all along. They have seen the lights of settlements in the distance as they journeyed but the aboriginals must have been aiming for a specific one as their destination. So much have the two boys enjoyed their interlude with these people – with food, laughter and a strong sense of being looked after – that when they are left they feel very sad and lonely as if they are 'abandoned' or 'rejected'.

Hamlet (page 51)

1 (a) encrusted

(b) grievances

(c) gaudy

(d) contempt

(e) dispensed

(f) forsake

2 It is two months since the death of her husband as the result of a snake bite when he was asleep in his orchard. The widowed queen is now Queen again because she has married her late husband's brother who has become the new King.

3 He must have been a good King. He was dearly loved and everyone in Denmark grieved when he died – but not for long.

4 The new King is strong and handsome. He seems to be physically attractive which may be why the queen has married him so quickly. He smiles a lot 'like a small coin of royal charity' which seems to suggest that his smiles may not be sincere. He deals with courtiers, politics and international affairs very efficiently and decisively but seems to be finding his new stepson difficult. 'Annoyance' is mentioned in connection with Hamlet and he will not let him return to school at Wittenberg.

5 The rest of the court is now wearing 'a sea of bright colour' for the new King's coronation but Hamlet is a 'young man in black' so we infer that he is registering an objection to the court's being no longer in mourning for the old King, his father. He makes it clear he has no time for his new stepfather (and uncle) by muttering under his breath 'A little more than kin, and less than kind' and by shooting the older man a look of 'dislike and contempt'. He doesn't seem to take any notice of his worried mother when she asks him to cheer up and wear different clothes or 'to forsake his dark looks and attire'. He seems, in fact, be as scornful of her as he is of the

King. When he is left alone he looks even more coldly angry, making it clear that he regards the relationship between his mother and uncle as lustful and wrong.

The good wife and the bad husband (page 54)

1 (a) miserly, mean
   (b) rogue, villain, crook, con-man, thief
   (c) booty, spoils

2 First she is 'stupid' and 'gullible' by nature. Second she is susceptible to flattery and the con-man refers to her 'lovely heart'. Third she knows how mean her husband is so she doesn't find it hard to believe that he would neglect his elderly parents.

3 He is younger and better able to climb quickly and easily. The husband can climb only 'laboriously' and 'clumsily' but the thief can speedily jump between branches to make a rapid descent. He therefore has the advantage of speed and can use it to steal the horse and escape while the owner is still fumbling about in the tree.

4 He has not bothered to tell her that his parents are dead so that she believes it when told by a stranger that they are lonely and in need. At the end of the story he lies to her – or at least lets her make incorrect assumptions – by telling her that he has sent his horse to his father. He still doesn't admit that his parents are deceased. There appears to be no trust or confidence between them.

5 It shows that he is not only mean but that he is also concerned about how others see him – even his wife. He has been stupid and outwitted by a clever villain but he prefers to pretend that he was doing something virtuous for others. So he's an unpleasantly proud man.

6 An open-ended question open to a wide range of answers such as:
   The wife is good in that she is kind and generous to anyone who asks her for help – but surely this is offset by her stupidity. We're told that she repeatedly does this 'and always gave them money' so she doesn't learn even her mistakes. It's odd too, if this keeps happening, that she continues to be surprised by her husband's reaction. He is certainly a 'bad' husband (he is miserly and lies to his wife) but it's also understandable that he gets cross with his silly wife. 'The gullible wife and the impatient husband' might be a more accurate title although it's much less direct.

Cranford (page 57)

1 First they had tea and then they played cards.

2 (a) Filigree is very fine, elaborate metalwork consisting of tiny threads of metal which looks like metallic netting.
   (b) very small
   (c) shown or demonstrated

3 It seems to have been held in Lady Glenmire's honour. (It is clear that the narrator and her friends are not used to taking tea with someone who has a title [a peeress] and who has seen the Queen. We know that they are inhibited by her at first because after tea they relaxed and the narrator says 'we thawed into common-life subjects.')

4 It is a slightly witty, ironic way of saying that the people of Cranford had been so apprehensive about meeting Lady Glenmire that they had discussed at length amongst themselves how they should address a noblewoman with appropriate etiquette.

5 First, she is mean. The sugar is in tiny pieces and the tongs too small to pick up more than one piece. By implication she is mean about other things too because sugar is just her 'favourite economy'. Second, she is besotted with her pet, Carlo, to such an extent that she is prepared to be discourteous to guests in order to give him treats.

6 (a) There is cream on the table and the guests are silently put out when Mrs Jamieson pours it all into a saucer with tea for Carlo – by inference a dog – to enjoy. This leaves the guests feeling envious and inwardly a bit cross when they are told by Mrs Jamieson to 'admire the gratitude' when Carlo wags his tail. They are also disappointed by the 'very thin' bread and butter, and the 'very small' lumps of sugar.
   (b) The guests are pleased when Lady Glenmire orders extra bread and butter.

7 She has been at the royal court – the circle around the royal family – in London and has been in the presence of the Queen. She is approachable and seems to be comfortable chatting with the guests about subjects other than her experiences at court. She is sensitive to the needs of others and presumably doesn't mind showing that she too is hungry – hence the order for the extra bread and butter. She does not stand on ceremony and once the group gets involved in the three card games (Preference, Ombre and Quadrille) no one, not even the deferential Miss Pole, bothers to address her formally as 'my lady' or 'your ladyship'.

Watching the Tree (page 60)

1 (a) Shanghai
   (b) Hong Kong

2 (a) cynicism
   (b) censoring
   (c) psychologist
   (d) crucial (or pivotal)

3 He loved books and often referred to the *I Ching* (a famous Chinese classical text which gives advice about how to live). He was also artistically talented and spent time creating elaborate Chinese lettering in the traditional way by grinding an ink stick on a stone slab to create ink. He was kind to the author who, in infancy, would play on the balcony opening from his room. Sometimes he let her help although she inherited no talent for calligraphy. By profession the grandfather was a businessman.

4 She was the youngest stepdaughter in a family of seven and made to feel like 'a piece of garbage' by her cruel stepmother who ensured that she felt rejected and unwanted. Only her Ye Ye and her aunt were kind and nurturing to her. When she was ten her stepmother sent her away to a string of different boarding schools and she was allowed home only three times in four years so she felt very lonely, miserable ('At times things were very bad') and isolated. Her letters were controlled by her parents and she had no communication with the aunt she loved throughout the four years she was away at school.

5 Her grandfather made the author feel that she was loved and that she mattered. He gave her an essential

sense of basic trust by showing her that there was someone in her life who cared. Without him she implies, in agreement with Swedish psychologist Eric Ericson, she would have died mentally because a child cannot live without that trust. As it was, she could think of her grandfather and it would 'revive my spirits at odd moments'. Although she didn't work all this out for many years, she is convinced, with hindsight, that her Ye Ye was 'pivotal' in her development into the adult she eventually became.

Great Expectations (page 63)

1 It is about a mile from the village Pip lives in to the church.
2 Joe Gargery is a blacksmith or metal worker.
3 The man wants to frighten Pip as much as he can because he needs things which Pip can provide. He also wants to see if Pip has anything useful in his pockets.
4 The man who terrifies Pip has clearly suffered and struggled. He is very muddy and his feet are injured where he has walked over rough ground, been cut by stones, stung by nettles and scratched by branches. His movements are very limited because his leg is locked to 'a great iron' – a device used to hobble prisoners and prevent their escape. He is also wet and cold, and is shivering. His clothes are grey; he has a rag tied around his head instead of a hat and his shoes are damaged. He growls and shouts at Pip. Although Pip doesn't have the experience to work it out, Dickens makes it clear to the reader via the leg iron and the coarse clothing that this man is a prisoner on the run.
5 The man wants food because he is very hungry. He eats the crust which falls from Pip's pocket 'ravenously' and demands that Pip bring him further 'wittles' from home later. Then, when he learns that Pip lives with a metal worker he tells him to bring a file. He doesn't say what he plans to do with it but perhaps he wants to remove the shackle from his leg because with a file you can rub away metal.
6 (a) nervously
    (b) dead
    (c) listen
7 Pip is an orphan. His father and his mother, Georgiana, are both buried in the churchyard near where he and his assailant are standing. Pip lives with his adult sister who is married to the village blacksmith, Joe Gargery.

The Cataract of Lodore (page 66)

1 The source is on higher ground ('on the fell'). The poet also refers to this as 'its fountains/In the mountains'.
2 It flows gently downhill though mossy land, reeds, meadows and woodlands as it gradually builds up in volume and speed. At one point it reaches flatter country and forms a 'little lake' in which it 'sleeps' before 'departing,/Awakening and starting' on its way to a steeper slope where it seems to be 'smoking and frothing'.
3 From many possibilities: 'leaping', 'hopping', 'brawling', 'grumbling', 'dancing'
4 He is stressing that the waterfall is 'A sight to delight in'. It astonishes him and fills him with awe. It is also very loud so that if you stand beside it, the sound is overpowering.
5 The rhyme – mostly words ending in 'ing' and the repetition of the word 'and' help to suggest the sound

of the water gathering momentum. If you read the poem aloud you can hear and feel the sound of the water moving ever faster. The rhyme, which isn't always regular, as the rill bubbles unevenly downhill, sometimes occurs at the end of lines ('around' and 'rebound' or 'bent' and descent') and often internally within lines ('shocking' and 'rocking' or 'whitening and brightening'). The relentlessness of this helps to reinforce the idea that the water is 'so never ending, but always descending'.
6 Each section uses longer lines, with more syllables, than the previous one. By the time the poet gets to the final section most of the lines have four verbs (such as 'advancing', 'prancing', 'glancing', 'dancing') separated by four uses of 'and', making twelve syllables. In the first and second stanzas most lines have only five syllables. This breathless technique helps to create the effect of the water gathering momentum.

Adders (page 69)

1 Chemicals sprayed on crops to kill insects have killed adders. They cannot live easily in places affected by industrial pollution and emissions from traffic, aircraft, and so on. Also, many adders have been deliberately killed by human beings who mistakenly regard them as dangerous.
2 The writer saw an adder on a footpath in a National Park in the north of England on a chilly summer's day and in a tree-surrounded lake in the south of England on a very hot summer day.
3 Reptiles cannot create their own body warmth or cool their bodies internally as mammals do. Instead they have to absorb warmth from the sun in the mornings, which is why they tend to be slow and inactive until they have built up enough energy from the sun's rays to let them move more quickly. If it gets too hot they need to cool themselves down by, for example, getting into water.
4 They mate in early summer. Instead of laying her eggs like a bird, the female adder keeps them inside her body until they are ready to hatch when the young, usually about ten of them, wriggle out of her, alive. This mechanism protects them from the weather.
5 It is very efficient. The animal has jaw bones which swivel. Attached to these are hollow fangs. The poison passes into the fangs from ducts as the snake strikes and the jaws move into position. Every drop of venom is neatly injected into the victim.
6 First, you might get bitten, which is painful, means a visit to hospital and can, very occasionally, prove fatal. Second, it is against the law. Adders are a protected species and have been since 1981.

The Voices at the Window (page 72)

1 It was autumn and, after dusk, the temperature dropped. It was also raining. The nobleman was both very cold and very wet.
2 The huntsman chopped down the apple tree to prevent his master from eating the fruit. He polluted the water in the stream by turning it to blood with his sword so that the nobleman couldn't drink from it. He used his sword to turn the bed to coal before his employer could

lie on it. These three actions, all involving a sword, saved the other man's life three times.

3 The huntsman knew, or at least hoped, that when he revealed the truth it would be the horse that was turned to stone rather than him if he was mounted on it. Since the horse would be, effectively, killed by being turned to stone he chose one which was already at the end of its useful life rather than wasting a good horse.

4 The nobleman made a promise that once he and the other men were sheltered, warm and fed they would while away the night by telling stories. Instead they ate and drank and then fell asleep. The voices were, presumably, angry because they wanted to hear the stories.

5 (a) prophesied, prognosticated
   (b) enticing, inviting, beguiling, appealing, alluring

6 Thrice-thwarted means that he had been denied what he wanted three times.

7 It begins 'Once upon a time' and none of the characters has a name but each is known by what he is – a nobleman or a huntsman. Things happen in threes: three voices, three curses and three levels of punishment (compare this with, for example, 'The Three Bears', 'The Three Little Pigs' and many stories that feature three wishes). The language is generally direct and mostly quite simple (for example 'It did not go well for them', 'In the morning, the hunting party set off for home'). The story is repetitive – as the three voices come to the window in turn and as the huntsman takes his preventative action on the way home. It includes magic, curses and punishments. It has moral messages: if you are loyal to your boss you will find a way of saving yourself because you've done right even though he may misunderstand you. It also suggests that you should keep your promises.

The Child's Elephant (page 75)

1 The author mentions cicadas, a bush rat, a herd-boy and long yellow grass as she sets her scene in the first paragraph.

2 He is seven and he seems to be alone out on the savannah in charge of the grazing cattle.

3 He has heard a gun shot nearby and he is frightened because he doesn't know who has fired the rifle or why. So he sinks down in the grass, which is taller than he is, like a bird needing cover, and he keeps absolutely still, knees clasped and hands over his mouth, as a way of protecting himself. He knows that he will have to find out what has happened but his initial reaction is to hide in safety.

4 He feels vulnerable, fearing that 'every glint of the light could have been a stranger's glance' and that someone is creeping up on him. He has heard voices and laughter nearby which have 'sent flurries of nerves stirring across his bare flesh'. It is the unbearable tension ('uncertainty') that eventually leads him to emerge so that he can investigate.

5 The cattle are grazing on the grasses which they pull at with long tongues. The herd includes at least one very young calf which is still suckling. When the rifle shot is heard the beasts stop eating and look up. Then when they realise that there is no threat to them they return, 'peaceable' and 'undisturbed', to their munching.

6 (a) cicadas, bush rat, lizard, sandgrouse (The cattle and chicken are domestic rather than wild.)
   (b) Campbell-Johnston uses them to reinforce the atmosphere of the African savannah so that we can hear, see and almost touch the creatures Bat lives alongside. She also wants us to enter into Bat's consciousness and experience. He lives very close to nature and these sounds and sights – although they're disrupted here by the rifle shot – are part of his everyday world. The lizard, in particular, with its 'skinny brown tail' and the 'gold-ringed bead of its eye' is as still as Bat but then darts off and adds real colour and authenticity to the description. When he makes a comparison such as 'still as a sandgrouse' it comes naturally to Bat – as the author describes his thoughts – to liken himself to a creature with which he's familiar.

The Morning Gift (page 78)

1 (a) It is cold and wet, more like winter than spring.
   (b) Ruth is very panicky, anxious and unhappy about what she is going to do and the chilly weather is a reflection of that. She even empathises with the miserable pigeons outside.

2 She seems to be in a museum – presumably as a temporary place to stay (she has slept on a camp bed and has only the cloakroom tap to wash at). The author mentions fossil-bearing rocks, stuffed animals and dinosaur bones. By implication she is a research worker at the museum – that's who the green soap she uses is meant for. She has brought her clothes from 'the flat' and seems to have spent the night camped in some kind of office at the museum.

3 She is going to wear a thick woollen skirt (probably green) and a woollen sweater.

4 She would rather have been marrying Heini. She would have worn a pretty white dress and carried flowers on her way across the lake to the church with its onion dome. All her family, including eccentric aunts and uncles, would have been there. In church she would have been presented by her father to curly-headed, sweet smiling Heini.

5 He is a pianist who had played his first major concert in Vienna's most prestigious concert hall, The Musikverein with the (Vienna) Philharmonic. Ruth had worn a dark brown velvet dress – the same colour as the piano (Bechstein) – to turn his pages.

6 Vienna is now very troubled. The windows of Ruth's grandfather's shop have been smashed and people forbidden to shop there. She seems to be hiding in a museum. Her people are being persecuted. Ruth is, very reluctantly, marrying the wrong man now as a way of escaping so that at some point in the future she and Heini will be able to get together again.

7 He too must work at the museum if he has keys. He is silent – so presumably there is a need to be careful and secretive. He has arranged this carefully with Ruth because she is ready when he arrives.

(b) Anna Murgatroyd?

_____

_____

_____ (2)

5 Considering the work of the children in this show, what does the writer

  (a) like

_____

_____

_____

_____

_____

_____

_____ (5)

  (b) find fault with?

_____

_____

_____

_____

_____ (4)

6 Summarise in your own words what she liked about the music.

_____

_____

_____

_____

_____

_____

_____ (6)

Wind and rain

This article by journalist Sara Smyth comes from *Daily Mail*, Tuesday 22 October 2013.

Half-term to be hit by wind and rain

Flood warnings have been issued for parts of Britain as heavy rain and high winds are expected to hit the country over the next ten days.

The Environment Agency said areas in south-west England, the Midlands and Wales were at risk of flooding, despite breaks in the wet weather.

In Wales, residents in ten areas have been advised to be vigilant amid predictions that the heavy rainfall and flash flooding that began over the weekend, is set to continue.

The warnings come after roads and shops in Cardiff were closed on Saturday because of the treacherous weather and blustery conditions.

The gloomy forecast is likely to disrupt families during next week's half-term holidays. Severe warnings are in place for the central, Tayside and Fife area, south-west Scotland, Lothian, Strathclyde and Borders and south-west England as well as Wales.

A Met Office spokesman said: 'The west will see the heaviest rain today. By the end of the day the band of rain will spread across the country. Over the next 15 days, trends show that there could be strong winds and possible gales in the north and west.'

However, forecasters say there could be a break in the rain mid-week, reducing the flooding risk in south-west England.

Chris Burton, forecaster with MeteoGroup, said: 'When you look for the next ten days it is going to stay unsettled.

'There will be heavy rain at times and quite strong westerly winds at times but there will be some dry spells. I think Wednesday into Thursday looks quite dry for most areas with more rain moving in on Friday. It is a mobile weather picture at the moment.'

The heaviest rain so far this week was in Boscombe Down, Wiltshire, where 1.4in (35mm) fell in 24 hours. Natural Resources Wales said it was asking people to be vigilant for localised flooding. 'Following a wet weekend and heavy showers today, more persistent, heavy rain is forecast to move in overnight tonight and affect most parts of Wales throughout tomorrow morning,' a spokesman said.

The spokesman added: 'There is also a chance that smaller streams and ditches may not be able to cope with the heavy rain, causing localised flooding.'

From an article by Sara Smyth in *Daily Mail* (2013)

Exercise •

1 Which areas are likely to experience flooding?

_____

_____

_____ (3)

2 Which areas are *not* likely to have the worst weather?

_____

_____

_____ (2)

3 Why is the forecast particularly bad news for families?

_____

_____

_____

_____ (3)

4 Give another word or phrase for

(a) vigilant

_____ (1)

(b) treacherous.

_____ (1)

5 Find two words in the passage which mean 'changeable'.

_____ (2)

6 Summarise the weather forecast for the next ten days in a single sentence.

_____

_____

_____

_____ (4)

7 (a) Which two organisations does the journalist refer to at the end of the passage?

_____

_____

_____

_____ (2)

(b) Why does she include them?

_____

_____

_____

_____

_____

_____

_____

_____

_____

_____

_____

_____

_____

_____

_____ (7)

> Use, in your answers, an accurate term for the writer of the
> text such as novelist, author, poet, journalist or biographer.

Please Miss We're Boys

Susan Elkin describes one of the pupils in her first class in a Deptford all-boys school in 1968.

Wonderfully named Bartholomew Paradise was part of a large Jamaican family who lived in the flats in nearby Tidemill Road. He was delightful – courteous, friendly and conscientious. Diligent and bright, he got on very well with his classmates, always had a smile for me and plenty of sensible things to say in class discussions.

But he never came to school on Monday mornings, which puzzled me for several weeks. Casual – and strangely regular – truancy just didn't seem to fit in with the rest of his personality. His parents were salt-of-the-earth, evangelical Christians and his older brothers were all spoken highly of by staff at Creekside Comp who remembered them. Bartholomew was the youngest in the family and I suspect he was also the most intelligent.

In the end, I tackled him gently about those missing Monday mornings. He looked a bit troubled. 'Well, Miss,' he said. 'I come to school as soon as I can but it depends what time the rent man comes and sometimes he's late.'

The Paradise family, it transpired, paid their rent weekly, in cash and on the nail. This was long before the days of automatic bank transfers and I doubt that they had a bank account anyway. All Bartholomew's family worked hard and long hours, including his mother who, along with his father and elder siblings, would have been paid in cash on Friday evenings. For this family, getting into debt or owing money would have been unthinkable.

So when the rent man made his regular Monday morning call, as far as Mr and Mrs Paradise were concerned, someone had to be there to hand over the money. And because everyone else was at work, the job fell to Bartholomew.

Yes, the Paradise family valued education, but nothing was more important than paying the rent. It was a situation totally unlike anything I'd ever experienced with my grammar school friends, in my own family or social circle, but how could I argue? Of course, they were technically breaking the law. It was 'condoned truancy' after all. But their motives were so inarguably laudable that I turned a blind eye – as did the school's Education Welfare Officer when I explained the situation. Anyway Bartholomew worked so hard and sensibly at school for the rest of the time that he never fell behind.

From *Please Miss We're Boys* by Susan Elkin (2013)

1 Where does Bartholomew Paradise live?

_____

_____ (2)

2 Find words in the passage that mean the same as

   (a) hardworking

   _____ (1)

   (b) praiseworthy

   _____ (1)

   (c) turned out

   _____ (1)

   (d) permitted.

   _____ (1)

3 Why do Mr and Mrs Paradise not arrange to pay their rent in some other way?

   _____

   _____

   _____

   _____

   _____ (3)

4 Summarise what you learn from this passage about Bartholomew's parents.

   _____

   _____

   _____

   _____

   _____

   _____

   _____

   _____

   _____

   _____ (4)

5 What do you learn about Bartholomew from this passage?

_____

_____

_____

_____

_____

_____ (4)

6 (a) Explain why the writer is surprised by Bartholomew's situation.

_____

_____

_____

_____

_____

_____ (4)

(b) Explain how she responded to the problem of Bartholomew's absence.

_____

_____

_____

_____

_____

_____

_____

_____ (4)

Alone on a Wide Wide Sea

This extract comes from Michael Morpurgo's 2006 novel *Alone on a Wide Wide Sea*. The narrator, a 1940s British orphan, has been sent to an appalling children's slave camp in Australia. He and Marty have escaped and are being helped by Australian aboriginal people.

And the longer we were with them the more sure we became that these people were absolutely no threat to us. They might not talk to us. They might keep their distance. They might still stare at us more than we liked, but there was never the slightest hint of hostility towards us. On the contrary they seemed very protective of us, and as fascinated by us as we were by them. And the children found us endlessly funny, particularly when we smiled, so we smiled a lot. But then we felt like smiling. They shared their food with us: berries, roots, fruit and baked wallaby once. We had all the water we needed.

Marty did try once or twice to ask where we were going, but was simply given more fruit or berries as an answer. So he gave up. But up on Big Black Jack, as we rode through the night, or resting in the shade, the two of us speculated at length. Maybe we weren't being taken anywhere. I mean, they never looked as if they were going anywhere in particular. They just looked as if they were quite happy simply going, simply being. Or maybe they were adopting us into their tribe and we'd wander the bush with them for the rest of our lives. Maybe they were still making up their minds what to do with us. Perhaps we'd just wake up one day and find them gone. We really didn't mind. All we could be sure of was that we were a long, long way from Cooper's Station now, and further every day. Where we were going wasn't important. Sometimes at night we'd see lights in the distance, more settlements probably, but we never thought of running off. We were safe with them. We had no reason to leave them.

I can't say exactly how many days and nights our journey lasted – it could have been five or six days perhaps. I do know that it lasted long enough for Marty and I to begin to believe it might be permanent, that we had indeed been adopted in some way. I certainly was beginning to feel comfortable among them, not because they became any less reserved – they didn't. Distance seemed to be important to them. The children though were a different story. We very soon got beyond just smiling and laughing. We splashed each other in the pools. We skimmed stones, threw sticks, ambushed one another. One took to riding piggyback on Marty's back, and the smallest of them would often ride up with us on Big Black Jack loving every moment of it. We were finding our place among them, beginning to feel accepted. That's why, when our journey finally ended, we felt all the more abandoned, even rejected.

From *Alone on a Wide Wide Sea* by Michael Morpurgo (2006)

Exercise

1 (a) How long does the narrator's journey with Marty and the tribal people last?

_____ (1)

(b) What is Big Black Jack likely to be?

_____

_____ (2)

2 Explain the meaning of the following words as they are used in the passage:

(a) hostility

_____ (1)

(b) speculated

_____ (1)

(c) reserved

_____ (1)

(d) ambushed

_____ (1)

3 Summarise in your own words the behaviour of the tribal adults towards the boys they are taking with them.

_____

_____

_____

_____

_____

_____

_____

_____

_____

_____ (5)

4 In what ways are the children different from the adults?

_____

_____

_____

_____

_____

_____

_____ (4)

5 What were the boys' theories about the tribe's plans for them?

_____

_____

_____

_____

_____

_____

_____ (4)

6 Explain in your own words how the journey ends.

_____

_____

_____

_____

_____

_____

_____

_____

_____ (5)

Hamlet

Hamlet is one of William Shakespeare's most famous plays and was written in about 1601. This extract is from a retelling by Leon Garfield in 1985.

The King, the great, good King, loved and honoured by all, had been dead for two months. He had been stung by a serpent while sleeping in his orchard, and all Denmark had wept. But now the time for grieving was past: sad eyes gave way to merry ones, long faces to round smiles; and the heavy black of mourning, that had bandaged up the court, was washed away by a sea of bright colour. Yellow silks and sky-blue satins, encrusted with silver, blazed in the ceremonial chamber, and the walls were hung with glory. There was a new King – even though there was still the same Queen. She had married again, and with her dead husband's brother.

This new King was a sturdy gentleman, broad-shouldered and broad-featured, and much given to smiling – as well he might, for he had gained a luxurious throne and a luxurious queen at a stroke. Affably he conducted the affairs of state, dispatching ambassadors to Norway to patch up grievances and giving gracious permission to Laertes, his faithful chamberlain's son, to return to France whence he'd come to attend the coronation. Next, still smiling, and with his strong hand guarding the jewelled hand of his Queen, he turned to her son, Prince Hamlet, a young man in black, like a plain thought in a gaudy world.

'But now, my cousin Hamlet, and my son –'

'A little more than kin, and less than kind,' murmured the Prince, with a look of dislike and contempt.

Anxiously the Queen, his mother, begged him to forsake his dark looks and dark attire. He answered her with scarcely more courtesy than he had shown the King. The King, hiding his annoyance, added his own urgings; and the young man submitted – to the extent to agreeing to remain at court and not return to school at Wittenberg as he had wished. The King was satisfied and, with more smiles (which he dispensed like the small coin of royal charity), he left the chamber with the backward-glancing Queen upon his arm. As if on apron-strings, the crowded courtiers followed.

Hamlet was alone. Long and hard he stared after the departed court. The look upon his face, had it been seen by the royal pair who had inspired it, would have chilled their hearts, made stone of their smiles, and poison of the lust of their bed.

From *Shakespeare Stories* by Leon Garfield (1985)

Exercise ●●●●●●●●●●●●●●●●●●●●●●●●●●●●

1 Find words in the passage that mean

   (a) thickly decorated with

   _____ (1)

   (b) disputes

   _____ (1)

   (c) scruffily colourful

   _____ (1)

   (d) disdain

   _____ (1)

   (e) gave out

   _____ (1)

   (f) give up.

   _____ (1)

2 Explain how the Queen's circumstances have changed in the last two months.

   _____

   _____

   _____

   _____

   _____

   _____ (4)

3 What do you learn about the old King from this passage?

   _____

   _____

   _____

   _____

   _____ (4)

4 Summarise in your own words what this passage tells you about the new King.

_____

_____

_____

_____

_____

_____

_____

_____ (5)

5 What is Hamlet's attitude to the situation he now finds himself in?

_____

_____

_____

_____

_____

_____

_____

_____

_____

_____

_____

_____

_____

_____ (6)

Use phrases such as 'the author suggests' or 'we can infer' or 'by inference' in your answers.

The good wife and the bad husband

This is a traditional or folk story from South India, retold by Susan Elkin.

Once upon a time a stupid, gullible woman lived with her rich, but miserly, husband in a remote village in India.

Cunning beggars often went to the woman and spun her sob stories. They also paid her compliments. She always gave them money behind her husband's back and when he found out he grew very angry.

One day a rogue came to her while her husband was out and said: 'I live in Kailasa. Your husband's parents live near me and I've come to tell you that they are very poor. They have hardly any clothes and nothing to eat. It would break your lovely heart to see them.'

Now, it so happens that the woman's in-laws had died a long time before this but her husband hadn't told her.

In her ignorance, and flattered by her visitor's oily manner, she gave the man all the clothes that she and her husband owned. Then she gave him her jewel box. Finally she also thrust at the man the entire contents of her husband's cash chest.

When the husband arrived home later that day she excitedly told him what she had done, foolishly expecting him to be delighted. Of course he was absolutely furious.

Calming himself later, he made his wife tell him which way the villain had gone and followed him. Eventually he caught up with the man who had all his booty wrapped up in his coat. Realising he was likely to be caught the thief shinned up a tree.

'Come down at once,' shouted the husband standing at the foot of the tree, his horse tied to another tree nearby.

Of course the con-man would not, so after a while the husband began laboriously to climb the tree. But the crook was younger and more agile. He hopped from branch to branch and quickly reached the ground while the husband was still clumsily trying to reach him.

The younger man then leaped on to the other's horse and escaped at top speed with his spoils.

When the husband arrived home without his horse he felt very silly. But rather than admit what had happened he let his wife think that he had sent his horse to Kailasa to be used by his father.

The message of this story is that some mean people who never help others will pretend to have done so when they happen to lose something by accident or stupidity.

Exercise

1 (a) Which two adjectives in this story indicate that the husband was ungenerous to others?

_____

_____ (1)

(b) List five nouns used in this story which mean the same as criminal.

_____

_____ (1)

(c) Find two words used here to mean stolen goods.

_____

_____ (1)

2 Why do you think the woman is so quick to believe that her in-laws are alone and poor? There are at least three reasons.

_____

_____

_____

_____

_____ (4)

3 What advantage does the thief have over the husband?

_____

_____

_____

_____

_____ (4)

4 What indications are there in this story that the husband does not talk to his wife and share things with her?

_____

_____

_____

_____

_____

_____

_____ (4)

5 What does the lie at the end of the story show about the husband?

_____

_____

_____

_____

_____ (4)

6 How appropriate do you think the title of this story is?

_____

_____

_____

_____

_____

_____

_____

_____

_____

_____

_____ (6)

Cranford

Cranford by Elizabeth Gaskell is about small-town life early in the nineteenth century. Much of it was drawn from the author's own experiences as a young woman.

'Oh!' said Mrs Jamieson, 'Lady Glenmire rang the bell; I believe it was for tea.'

In a few minutes tea was brought. Very delicate was the china, very old the plate, very thin the bread and butter, and very small the lumps of sugar. Sugar was evidently Mrs Jamieson's favourite economy. I question if the little filigree sugar-tongs, made something like scissors, could have opened themselves wide enough to take up an honest, vulgar good-sized piece; and when I tried to seize two little minnikin pieces at once, so as not to be detected in too many returns to the sugar-basin, they absolutely dropped one, with a little sharp clatter, quite in a malicious and unnatural manner. But before this happened we had had a slight disappointment. In the little silver jug was cream, in the larger one was milk. As soon as Mr Mulliner came in, Carlo began to beg, which was a thing our manners forbade us to do, though I am sure we were just as hungry; and Mrs Jamieson said she was certain we would excuse her if she gave her poor dumb Carlo his tea first. She accordingly mixed a saucerful for him, and put it down for him to lap; and then she told us how intelligent and sensible the dear little fellow was; he knew cream quite well, and constantly refused tea with only milk in it: so the milk was left for us; but we silently thought we were quite as intelligent and sensible as Carlo, and felt as if insult were added to injury when we were called upon to admire the gratitude evinced by his wagging his tail for the cream which should have been ours.

After tea we thawed down into common-life subjects. We were thankful to Lady Glenmire for having proposed some more bread and butter, and this mutual want made us better acquainted with her than we should ever have been with talking about the Court, though Miss Pole did say she had hoped to know how the dear Queen was from some one who had seen her.

The friendship begun over bread and butter extended on to cards. Lady Glenmire played Preference to admiration, and was a complete authority as to Ombre and Quadrille. Even Miss Pole quite forgot to say 'my lady', and 'your ladyship', and said 'Basto! ma'am'; 'you have Spadille, I believe', just as quietly as if we had never held the great Cranford Parliament on the subject of the proper mode of addressing a peeress.

From *Cranford* by Elizabeth Gaskell (1851)

1 What two activities do the narrator and others experience with Lady Glenmire?

_____

_____ (2)

2 Explain the meaning of or give other words which mean the same as

(a) filigree

_____

_____ (1)

(b) minnikin

_____

_____ (1)

(c) evinced.

_____

_____ (1)

3 What seems to be the purpose of this tea party?

_____

_____ (2)

4 What is meant by 'the great Cranford Parliament on the subject of the proper mode of addressing a peeress'?

_____

_____

_____

_____

_____ (4)

5 What are the two main things you learn about Mrs Jamieson?

_____

_____

_____

_____

_____ (4)

6 (a) What disappoints the guests about the tea?

_____

_____

_____

_____

_____

_____

_____

_____ (3)

(b) What cheers them up?

_____

_____

_____ (2)

7 Summarise what you learn about Lady Glenmire from this passage.

_____

_____

_____

_____

_____

_____

_____

_____

_____

_____

_____

_____ (5)

Watching the Tree

In *Watching the Tree* a Chinese/American doctor, Adeline Yen Mah, describes her beloved grandfather who helped her through a difficult childhood in China.

My grandfather (Ye Ye) and I shared a rapport that neither of us ever verbalised during his lifetime. He was a businessman but was more interested in books than money. As a little girl in Shanghai, I spent hours playing by myself on the balcony attached to his room. Through the French windows I could see him practising calligraphy, writing letters or consulting the *I Ching*. Sometimes, he would let me 'help' him make fresh ink by grinding the ink-stick on an antique stone slab left to him by his father. I did not inherit Ye Ye's artistic talent and was in awe of his *shu fa* (calligraphy).

As the youngest stepdaughter in a Chinese family of seven children, I knew I was unwanted and considered by my family to be the lowest of the low. At home, my misery filled my whole world. It was real and deep and I could see no way out, possessing neither the wisdom nor the cynicism to blunt the cruelty and the constant rejection.

When I was ten, my stepmother Niang separated me from my aunt, whom I dearly loved, and placed me in a succession of Catholic boarding schools. I was unaware that all my mail (both incoming and outgoing) was being sent to my parents for censoring. I only knew that I never heard from my aunt or anyone else for the next four years.

During that time I had nobody but my grandfather. Although I was only allowed 'home' on three separate occasions, I treasured those brief visits. I did not know then how vital they were to my emotional and spiritual development.

The Swedish psychologist Eric Ericson wrote of a sense of basic trust, which is instilled in a child by 'somebody who cares', without which the child cannot live and dies mentally. This 'basic trust' was what my Ye Ye gave to me at that crucial juncture. During the many years when I was isolated in the boarding school in Hong Kong, I was sustained only by my inner conviction that my Ye Ye loved me. At times, things were very bad. My stepmother had a way of making me feel like nothing; a piece of garbage to be thrown away. But, through it all, the thought of my Ye Ye would return and revive my spirits at odd moments. Deep inside, I knew I mattered to him and that he believed in me.

Many decades passed before I came to recognise the depth of his influence. His thoughts were pivotal in shaping me into the person I became.

From *Watching the Tree* by Adeline Yen Mah (2000)

Exercise •••••••••••••••••••••••••••••

1 (a) Where did the author grow up?

_____ (1)

(b) Where did she go to school?

_____ (1)

2 Find words in the passage that mean the same as

(a) contemptuous belief that others are no good

_____ (1)

(b) editing or withholding

_____ (1)

(c) someone who studies the working of the human mind

_____ (1)

(d) vitally important.

_____ (1)

3 What do you learn about her grandfather from the first paragraph?

_____

_____

_____

_____

_____

_____

_____

_____

_____

_____ (6)

4 In what ways was the author's childhood unhappy?

_____

_____

_____

_____

_____

_____

_____

_____

_____

_____ (6)

5 Summarise the influence of her grandfather on the author.

_____

_____

_____

_____

_____

_____

_____

_____

_____

_____ (7)

Great Expectations

At the beginning of *Great Expectations* by Charles Dickens, Pip is alone in the churchyard near his home on the Kent marshes when he gets a dreadful fright.

'Hold your noise!' cried a terrible voice, as a man started up from among the graves at the side of the church porch. 'Keep still, you little devil, or I'll cut your throat!'

A fearful man, all in coarse grey, with a great iron on his leg. A man with no hat, and with broken shoes, and with an old rag tied round his head. A man who had been soaked in water, and smothered in mud, and lamed by stones, and cut by flints, and stung by nettles, and torn by briars; who limped, and shivered, and glared and growled; and whose teeth chattered in his head as he seized me by the chin.

'O! Don't cut my throat, sir,' I pleaded in terror. 'Pray don't do it, sir.'

'Tell us your name!' said the man. 'Quick!'

'Pip, sir.'

'Once more,' said the man, staring at me. 'Give it mouth!'

'Pip. Pip, sir.'

'Show us where you live,' said the man. 'Point out the place!'

I pointed to where our village lay, on the flat in-shore among the alder-trees and pollards, a mile or more from the church.

The man, after looking at me for a moment, turned me upside down, and emptied my pockets. There was nothing in them but a piece of bread. When the church came to itself – for he was so sudden and strong that he made it go head over heels before me, and I saw the steeple under my feet – when the church came to itself, I say, I was seated on a high tombstone, trembling, while he ate the bread ravenously.

'Now lookee here!' said the man. 'Where is your mother?'

'There, sir!' said I.

He started, made a short run, and stopped and looked over his shoulder.

'There, sir!' I timidly explained. 'Also Georgiana. That's my mother.'

'Oh!' said he, coming back. 'And is that your father alonger your mother?'

'Yes, sir,' said I; 'him too; late of this parish.'

'Ha!' he muttered then, considering. 'Who d'ye live with – supposin' you're kindly let to live, which I han't made up my mind about?'

'My sister, sir – Mrs Joe Gargery – wife of Joe Gargery, the blacksmith, sir.'

'Blacksmith, eh?' said he. And looking down at his leg and me several times, he came closer to my tombstone, took me by both arms, and tilted me back as far as he could hold me; so that his eyes looked most powerfully down into mine, and mine looked most helplessly into his.

'Now lookee here,' he said, 'the question being whether you're to be let to live. You know what a file is?'

'Yes, sir.'

'And you know what wittles is?'

'Yes, sir.'

After each question he tilted me over a little more, so as to give me a greater sense of helplessness and danger.

'You get me a file.' He tilted me again. 'And you get me wittles.' He tilted me again. 'You bring 'em both to me.' He tilted me again. 'Or I'll have your heart and liver out.' He tilted me again.

I was dreadfully frightened, and so giddy that I clung to him with both hands, and said 'If you would kindly please to let me keep upright, sir, perhaps I shouldn't be sick, and perhaps I could attend more.'

Abridged from *Great Expectations* by Charles Dickens (1861)

Wittles: the man's way of saying vittles or victuals, an old fashioned word for food.

Exercise •

1 How far is Pip's home from the churchyard?

_____ (2)

2 What does Pip's brother-in-law do for a living?

_____ (1)

3 Why does the 'fearful' man seize Pip and turn him upside down?

_____

_____

_____ (3)

4 Describe the man as fully as you can. Use your own words.

_____

_____

_____

_____

_____

_____

_____

_____ (6)

5 What does he want Pip to bring him and why?

_____

_____

_____

_____ (6)

6 Give another word or phrase for these words as they are used in the passage:

  (a) timidly

_____ (1)

  (b) late

_____ (1)

  (c) attend

_____ (1)

7 What do you learn about Pip's family from this passage?

_____

_____

_____ (4)

> Refer to the author by his or her surname. So it's
> Dickens (not Charles) and Gardner (not Sally).

The Cataract of Lodore

'The Cataract of Lodore' was written by Robert Southey in 1820 for his children. The poem describes a river with waterfalls near Derwentwater in Cumbria. Southey was Poet Laureate, a poet appointed by the King or Queen to write poems to mark special events.

From its sources which well
In the tarn on the fell;
From its fountains
In the mountains,
Its rills and its gills;
Through moss and through brake,
It runs and it creeps
For a while, till it sleeps
In its own little lake.
And thence at departing,
Awakening and starting,
It runs through the reeds,
And away it proceeds,
Through meadow and glade,
In sun and in shade,
And through the wood-shelter,
Among crags in its flurry,
Helter-skelter
Hurry-scurry.
Here it comes sparkling,
And there it lies darkling;
Now smoking and frothing
Its tumult and wrath in,
Till, in this rapid race
On which it is bent,
It reaches the place
Of its steep descent.

The cataract strong
Then plunges along,
Striking and raging
As if a war waging
Its caverns and rocks among;
Rising and leaping,
Sinking and creeping,

Swelling and sweeping,
Showering and springing,
Flying and flinging,
Writhing and ringing,
Eddying and whisking.
Spouting and frisking,
Turning and twisting,
Around and around
With endless rebound:
Smiting and fighting,
A sight to delight in;
Confounding, astounding,
Dizzying and deafening the ear with its sound.

Collecting, projecting,
Receding and speeding,
And shocking and rocking,
And darting and parting,
And threading and spreading,
And whizzing and hissing,
And dripping and skipping,
And hitting and splitting,
And shining and twining,
And rattling and battling,
And shaking and quaking,
And pouring and roaring,
And waving and raving,
And tossing and crossing,
And flowing and going,
And running and stunning,
And foaming and roaming,
And dinning and spinning,
And dropping and hopping,
And working and jerking,

And guggling and struggling,
And heaving and cleaving,
And moaning and groaning;

And glittering and frittering,
And gathering and feathering,
And whitening and brightening,
And quivering and shivering,
And hurrying and scurrying,
And thundering and floundering;

Dividing and gliding and sliding,
And falling and brawling and sprawling,
And driving and riving and striving,
And sprinkling and twinkling and
wrinkling,
And sounding and bounding and
rounding,
And bubbling and troubling and
doubling.
And grumbling and rumbling and
tumbling,
And clattering and battering and
shattering;

Retreating and beating and meeting and
sheeting,

Delaying and straying and playing and
spraying,
Advancing and prancing and glancing and
dancing,
Recoiling, turmoiling, and toiling and
boiling,
And gleaming and streaming and
steaming and beaming,
And rushing and flushing and brushing
and gushing,
And flapping and rapping and clapping
and slapping,
And curling and whirling and purling and
twirling,
And thumping and plumping, and
bumping and jumping,
And dashing and flashing and splashing
and crashing;
And so never ending, but always
descending,
Sounds and motions for ever and ever are
blending
All at once and all o'er, with a mighty
uproar, –
And this way the water comes down at
Lodore.

From 'The Cataract of Lodore' by Robert Southey

Exercise ●

1 Where does the river (or rill) rise or start?

_____

_____ (2)

2 How does the river proceed on its journey before it reaches 'the place/Of its steep descent'?

_____

_____

_____

_____

_____

_____ (5)

3 The poet personifies the river by pretending that it has human feelings and behaviour. Give examples of three words or phrases which demonstrate this.

_____

_____ (3)

4 Explain in your own words what Southey means by 'Confounding, astounding,/Dizzying and deafening the ear with its sound'.

_____

_____

_____ (4)

5 How does the poet use rhyme and repetition?

_____

_____

_____

_____

_____

_____

_____ (6)

6 Look carefully at the six sections of the poem. How do they differ and why?

_____

_____

_____

_____

_____

_____

_____ (5)

Poetry is easier to make sense of when you hear it as well as see it. So read it aloud to yourself. Or, if that's not convenient, read it slowly and silently in your head as if you are reading it aloud.

Adders

Adders are very pretty creatures. In *A Midsummer Night's Dream*
Shakespeare calls them 'spotted snakes' with 'enamelled skin'.
Perhaps he'd seen them in the woods near Stratford-upon-Avon
in Warwickshire where he grew up.

Alas the adder (*viperus berus*) is now much less common than it was in the
sixteenth and early seventeenth centuries when Shakespeare might have seen
them. Pesticides and pollution have done their worst. And the poor beast doesn't
enjoy a very friendly public image. For a long time many people killed any adder
they saw.

Even so, the adder is our commonest reptile. There are thought to be about half
a million adders in Britain from Scotland to Cornwall, although not in Ireland.
The story about fifth-century St Patrick having cast the snakes out of Ireland
is nice but scientifically it's more likely that The Emerald Isle is just too wet to
sustain them.

I waited many years for my first glimpse of a live adder in its natural habitat. And
then, as luck would have it, I saw two within a few weeks of each other – although
they were at opposite ends of England. The first was at Kielder Water in the
Northumberland National Park on a cool August day. It was about two o'clock in
the afternoon and there was a bit of watery sunshine as I walked along a streamside
path. And there stretched out in front of me as straight as ruler was Mr – or more
probably Mrs – Adder. About eighteen inches long, it was reddish brown in colour
with a bright zigzag line running dramatically along its back.

It was in no hurry to move. It allowed my husband to move in with a camera
about three feet above its head before turning with slow reluctance and sliding off
into the undergrowth and making us feel guilty for disturbing its sunbathing. For
that's what it was doing. Reptiles have variable body temperature. Unlike mammals
they have no inbuilt 'thermostat'. So they are very inactive until they've absorbed
enough warmth from the sun to get them going. Only then are they able to hunt the
small mammals, lizards, birds and eggs that they live on.

My second adder was at Bedgebury Pinetum, near Tonbridge in Kent in very
different weather. It was blisteringly hot and the adder had gone into the lake
for a cooling swim. Reptiles need warmth but they can't afford to overheat. It
was swimming happily along, its tiny delicate head held aloft and its muscular
body spiralling along behind to provide the forward momentum. It was a
lovely sight.

Adders are viviparous, which means that, instead of depositing them, the female
retains her eggs inside the body until they are ready to hatch. Because the eggs are
protected the adder can live and breed in northern climates which have only a short
summer season. Mating takes place in May or June. Then an average of ten young
are 'born' to each female in midsummer.

So what about the danger? The truth is there isn't much. Only fourteen people died of adder bite in Britain during the entire twentieth century, which means you're about as likely to die from it as you are to be hit by a meteorite. No adder goes looking for human beings to bite and it will attack only if you're silly enough to pick it up or provoke it. There have been cases of people being bitten after accidentally stepping or sitting on adders while out in the countryside, and of course if this happens it will hurt a lot and the victim must be taken to hospital for treatment immediately. Children, the elderly and the already sick are more likely to be dangerously affected by the venom, which works on the nervous system, than adults in reasonable health.

Actually, the mechanism of the bite is interesting. Two hollow fangs are fixed to a pair of rotating jaw bones and levered instantly into position as the animal strikes. Muscular contraction squeezes the poison along ducts into the fangs. It all goes into the victim or enemy as neatly as a jab at the doctor's. Not a drop is wasted.

Interfering with adders is obviously foolish. It's also illegal. The Wildlife and Countryside Act of 1981 gave legal protection to a wide range of animals and plants. Under Section 9 and Schedule 5 of the Act it is against the law to kill, injure, take, possess or sell an adder. Neither may you damage or destroy its place of shelter or protection.

So enjoy 'your' adder if you're lucky enough to spot one, but treat it with respect. 'It is the bright day that brings forth the adder,' Shakespeare makes Brutus say in *Julius Caesar*. Absolutely.

Exercise •

1 Why are adders less common now than they were in Shakespeare's time?

_____

_____

_____

_____

_____ (5)

2 Where and when did the writer observe her two adders?

_____

_____

_____

_____ (3)

3 How does the adder control its body temperature?

_____

_____

_____

_____

_____

_____

_____ (5)

4 How do adders breed?

_____

_____

_____

_____

_____ (4)

5 What is interesting about the way an adder bites?

_____

_____

_____

_____

_____ (4)

6 Give two reasons why you should not interfere with adders.

_____

_____

_____

_____

_____ (4)

> **You should write most of your comprehension answers in full sentences.**

The Voices at the Window

This story, 'The Voices at the Window', is a traditional or folk tale from Ukraine, retold here by Susan Elkin.

Once upon a time there was a nobleman who went hunting one autumn day with a party of huntsmen. It did not go well for them. At the end of the day they hadn't managed to kill a single deer. When night fell it got very cold and started to rain.

Wet through and with his teeth chattering, the nobleman said 'If only we had a warm hut, a white bed, soft bread and tea to drink we'd have nothing to complain of and we'd tell stories until dawn.'

Suddenly a light shone and all the nobleman's wishes were granted. They all went into the hut where they ate, drank and fell asleep – except for one man.

At about midnight the man heard a noise at the window. 'You have not kept your promise to tell tales until morning,' a voice said. 'So on the way home you will come to an irresistible tree full of apples but as soon as you taste them you will burst' it foretold.

When the cock crowed for the first time, as morning approached, a second voice came to the window: 'You have not kept your promise to tell tales until morning. So on the way home you will come, parched with thirst, to an enticing stream, but as soon as you taste its waters, you will burst,' it prophesied.

When it was almost light and the cock crowed a second time a third voice came to the window: 'You have not kept your promise to tell tales until morning. So on the way home, exhausted, you will come to an inviting feather bed but as soon as you lie on it you will burst,' it prognosticated.

The third voice added 'And if you tell any other man about these things you will be turned into stone up to the neck.'

In the morning, the hunting party set off for home. When they reached an appealing apple tree and the nobleman reached for an apple, the huntsman, quick as a flash, chopped the tree down with his sword. The apples turned to ashes.

When they reached an alluring stream and the nobleman was about to drink, the huntsman, quick as fire, plunged in his sword. The river turned to blood.

When they reached a beguiling bed and the nobleman was about to lie on it, the huntsman, quick as lightning, struck the bed with his sword. It turned to coals.

By now the thrice-thwarted nobleman was very angry and when they got home he summoned the huntsman to punish him. The huntsman arrived, mounted on a useless, very old horse. He told his master about the three voices at the window and what they had said.

As he spoke, the horse turned to stone to the knee, then to the breast and then to the neck – at which point the huntsman leaped off and asked the astonished nobleman, whose life he had saved three times, to pardon him.

Exercise ●

1 Why did the nobleman long for shelter and other comforts?

_____

_____

_____ (2)

2 What three quick actions did the huntsman take on the way home?

_____

_____

_____

_____

_____

_____

_____ (3)

3 Why did the huntsman choose an 'old and useless' horse at the end of the story?

_____

_____

_____

_____

_____

_____ (5)

4 Summarise in your own words why the voices were annoyed with the nobleman and his party.

_____

_____

_____

_____

_____ (4)

5 (a) Find two other verbs from the passage which mean the same as 'foretold'.

_____

_____ (2)

(b) Find five other adjectives from the passage which are similar in meaning to 'irresistible'.

_____

_____ (2)

6 Explain the meaning of 'thrice-thwarted'.

_____

_____ (2)

7 What features in this story make it clear, do you think, that this is traditional or folk tale?

_____

_____

_____

_____

_____

_____

_____

_____

_____

_____

_____

_____

_____

_____

_____

_____ (5)

> If you are asked for the meaning of a word in a comprehension exercise, look at the way it is used only in the context of the passage. Lots of words in English (think about 'volume', 'break' or 'work', for instance) have different meanings in different contexts.

The Child's Elephant

This is the opening of Rachel Campbell-Johnston's 2013 novel *The Child's Elephant*. It tells the story of an African village boy who raises an elephant calf whose mother has been killed. Later the boy becomes a boy soldier.

The sound of the rifle shot rang through the air. For a few moments it seemed as if the whole world had stopped. The cicadas fell silent, a bush rat dived for its burrow, the cattle paused in their chewing and looked upwards with empty stares; and Bat, the lone herd-boy who up till then had been dreaming, swishing at bushes with a long whippy branch, let the switch fall and dropped suddenly on his haunches. His head was quite hidden by the tall, yellow grass.

He felt the slow, rolling shudder through the soles of his feet. It rumbled his bones like the beat of the big tribal drum. Something that mattered had just happened out there on the savannah. He could feel it: something momentous that he didn't want to know about and yet knew at the same time he would have to find out. But not now, he thought, as he ducked even lower in the grasses. He let his breath leak through fingers clamped hard to his mouth. A lizard clung spellbound to a stalk right beside him. He gazed into the rapt gold-ringed bead of its eye. It stared back, unblinking, as if it had been stunned.

It seemed like for ever before the last fading echoes were finally quieted, before the waiting cicadas picked up their old song and the lizard, as if some bewitchment had suddenly been broken, darted off with a whisk of its skinny brown tail. In the shade of the thorn trees, the cattle returned to their grazing. They pulled at the grasses with long, curling tongues. But Bat, still as a sandgrouse that keeps low in its cover, hugged his arms around his knees and stayed down where he was.

He listened. Somewhere not so very far away he could hear people talking. The sound drifted like wood-smoke upon a slack wing: murmuring voices … then a clatter of laughter … the silence that followed it … then a sudden angry shout … then nothing again … then the bark of an order. The air carried the fragments in faint tattered snippets. They sent flurries of nerves stirring across his bare flesh.

Who was it? He could feel his pulse racing. His heart jumped in his throat. Every shift of the breeze could have been someone approaching; every glint of the light could have been a stranger's glance. Was someone even now stealing up upon him? Unable to bear the uncertainty, he rose to his feet.

Nothing looked very different. The cattle were peaceable; a new calf was suckling; the scrublands that stretched all about him looked quite undisturbed. It was funny how hiding played tricks with your imagination. He shouldn't have allowed himself to get so scared, he thought. He was seven after all: far to old to be behaving like some panicky chicken.

From *The Child's Elephant* by Rachel Campbell-Johnston (2013)

1 What details in the first paragraph make it clear that the story is set in Africa?

_____

_____

_____

_____ (2)

2 How old is Bat and what does his job seem to be?

_____

_____

_____ (2)

3 Explain in your own words why Bat 'stayed down where he was'.

_____

_____

_____

_____

_____

_____

_____

_____ (4)

4 What makes him emerge from hiding?

_____

_____

_____

_____

_____

_____

_____

_____

_____ (5)

5 What do you learn about the cattle Bat is guarding?

_____

_____

_____

_____

_____

_____ (3)

6 (a) List the different wild creatures mentioned in the passage.

_____

_____

_____ (2)

(b) Why does the author include them?

_____

_____

_____

_____

_____

_____

_____

_____

_____

_____

_____

_____

_____

_____ (7)

> Vary your verbs when you refer in your answers to an author's writing. He or she might hint, argue, declare, state, imply, include, describe, dismiss ... for example. Make your own list.

The Morning Gift

Eva Ibbotson's 2007 novel *The Morning Gift* tells the story of a
Jewish girl, Ruth, who marries Quin, an older Englishman, as a
way of escaping from the Germans before the Second World War.

It had rained since daybreak: slanting, cold-looking sheets of rain. Down in the square, the bedraggled pigeons huddled against Maria Theresia's verdigris skirts. Vienna, the occupied city, had turned its back on the spring.

Ruth had scarcely slept. Now she folded the blanket on the camp bed, washed as best she could under the cloakroom tap, brewed a cup of coffee.

'This is my wedding day,' she thought. 'This is the day I shall remember as I lie dying –' and felt panic seize her.

She had put her loden skirt and woollen sweater under newspaper, weighed down by a tray of fossil-bearing rocks, but this attempt at home-ironing had not been successful. Should she after all wear the dress she had bought for Heini's debut with the Philharmonic? She'd taken it from the flat and it hung now behind the door: brown velvet with a Puritan collar of heavy cream lace. It came from her grandfather's department store: the attendants had all come to help her choose; to share her pleasure in Heini's debut. Now the store had its windows smashed; notices warned customers not to shop there. Thank heaven her grandfather was dead.

No, that was Heini's dress – her page-turning dress, for it mattered what one wore to turn over music. One had to look nice, but unobtrusive. The dress was the colour of the Bechstein in the Musikverein – it had nothing to do with the Englishman who ran away from Strauss.

She wandered through the galleries and, in the grey light of dawn, her old friends, one by one, became visible. The polar bear, the elephant seal ... the ichthyosaurus with the fake vertebrae. And the infant aye-aye which she had restored to its case.

'Wish me luck,' she said to the ugly little beast, leaning her head against the glass.

She closed her eyes and the primates of Madagascar vanished as she saw the wedding she had planned so often with her mother. Not here, but on the Grundlsee, rowing across to the little onion-domed church in a boat – in a whole flotilla of boats, because everyone she loved would be there. Uncle Mishak would grumble a little because he had to dress up; Aunt Hilda would get stuck in her zip ... and the Zillers would play. 'On the landing stage,' Ruth had suggested, but Biberstein said no, he was too fat to play on a landing stage. She would wear white organdie and carry a posy of mountain flowers, and as she walked down the aisle on her father's arm, there would be Heini with his mop of curls and his sweet smile.

(Oh, Heini, forgive me. I'm doing this for us.)

Back in the cloakroom, she looked at her reflection once again. She had never seemed to herself so plain and unprepossessing. Suddenly she loosened her hair, filled the basin with cold water, seized the cake of green soap that the museum found adequate for its research workers ...

Quin, letting himself in silently, found her ready, her suitcase strapped.

From *The Morning Gift* by Eva Ibbotson (2007)

Exercise •

1 (a) Describe the weather.

_____

_____ (2)

(b) How does it suit Ruth's mood?

_____

_____

_____

_____

_____ (2)

2 What sort of building does Ruth seem to be in?

_____

_____

_____

_____

_____

_____

_____

_____

_____

_____

_____ (4)

3 What is she going to wear for her wedding?

_____

_____ (2)

4 Whom would she rather have been marrying and what would the wedding have been like?

_____

_____

_____

_____

_____

_____ (3)

5 What else do you learn about Heini from this passage?

_____

_____

_____

_____

_____ (3)

6 What do you think she means by 'Heini, forgive me. I'm doing this for us'?

_____

_____

_____

_____

_____

_____

_____ (5)

7 What do you deduce about Quin from the final sentence?

_____

_____

_____

_____ (4)

> Unless you're in an exam, always have a good dictionary at hand when you are working on a comprehension exercise.